The Road To Tyranny

Individualism to Collectivism

The Road To Tyranny

Individualism to Collectivism

Don Jans

ISBN 978-0-692-04863-4

SMEA Publishing

PREFACE

I came to learn that Americans from both sides of the political spectrum have a cursory understanding of many of the terms they use to describe philosophies with which they agree or those they condemn. For instance, those on the left choose to refer to anybody with whom they do not agree as a Nazi. The Nazi's are on the far left side of the political spectrum. The reason history refers to the Nazi's as being to the right is because they are just to the right of the Communists. The Nazi party in Germany viewed the German Communist Party as their main competition to the Nazi's desire for power and thus opposed them. Today people use Nazi to mean far right even though they were far left. People also use Communist, Socialist, and Progressive interchangeably. There are differences. For instance, Karl Marx who co-authored 'The Communist Manifesto' with his close associate Friedrich Engels, stated many times that he was not a Socialist. The differences between Communism, Socialism, and Progressives are miniscule compared to their many similarities.

During the question and answer segment of speaking engagements or as a guest on radio programs, I receive many questions that have brought me to the above conclusion. I have also learned that many people want to discuss the differences, not for the purpose of educating or drawing meaningful comparisons or differences, but instead to try to impress others. This, I have concluded is a waste of time and energy. The United States is on a dangerous trajectory, and it is far more important that trajectory be stopped and reversed than to be concerned with the hubris of any individual.

My purpose in writing this book is to draw clear distinctions between the forces that are dividing and destroying the United States today. Rather than getting bogged down by the subtle differences of the "isms" on the left, I chose to use the broad categories on the political spectrum; those being individualism and collectivism. It was also not my intent to limit this book to describing current political parties or specific individuals. The forces of individualism and collectivism transcend political parties and individuals.

It is important to note that the idea of writing a book on this topic came to me several years ago. Many outlines were drafted and discarded. It seemed I always descended into the quagmire of current political events, which is exactly what I did not want to do. That is when I decided that current political parties or individuals would not be used as examples or as a part of any discussion. My purpose is to explain the concepts of individualism and collectivism, how our founders viewed these concepts, and how these concepts have shaped and are shaping the United States today.

There are so many people that should be acknowledged that I am sure I will miss some. If I missed you, please understand it was not intentional. First, I must acknowledge my children. They have no idea how much they have contributed because they have no idea how many times I used them as sounding boards. Thank you, kids, for indulging me.

Many other people contributed by reading the book and then making corrections, by pointing to areas that needed clarification or enhancements, and by giving encouragement. Thank you, Fern Pham, Emily Krenick, Wayne Buck, Debbie Buck, Cyndi Tingey, Mark Roberts, and a very special thanks to my granddaughters Jadyn and Jillian Estrada who assisted with naming the book and designing the cover.

TABLE OF CONTENTS

Chapter 1. INDIVIDUALISM AND COLLECTIVISM

The story of the United States of America is a fascinating and captivating story. There is nothing like it in history. It began with people seeking different things. Those early settlers in Jamestown were seeking fortune. The Pilgrims that landed at Plymouth were seeking the right to worship God freely. Others came later seeking the same things, different things, or escaping from some hardship life had bestowed upon them. Because of circumstances, or was it destiny, the idea of freedom, liberty, and self-rule began. Americans determined they did not have to accept a certain station in life simply because of their status at birth. Americans also determined they did not have to accept demands by government if they did not have a direct input. That is how this great nation began. America became the land of opportunity, freedom, and liberty. The ideology of individualism had begun as opposed to the ideology of collectivism which advocates the control of mankind.

The dictionary definition of Individualism is the habit or principle of being independent and self-reliant and a social theory favoring freedom of action for individuals over collective or state control. Individualism is the belief and practice that every person is unique and self-reliant. A belief in individualism also implies that you believe that you can make decisions for yourself and the government has no place in your individual affairs or individual decisions.

Individualists, throughout history, have resented the interference of bureaucrats or government officials dictating to them how they should think, what is best for them, and how they should live their lives. The lives of people in early history were often dictated at birth. The individualist was told that he must accept his predestined lot in life regardless of his intellect, abilities, desires, or ambition. Periodically we would find examples of slaves or peasants rising above their birth dictated, society dictated, or government dictated life roles.

From slave to emperor – 10 remarkable rises to power from humble beginnings (1)

1. Diocletian (244 – 311 AD) – from slave to emperor

Diocletian was born as Diocles in the Roman province of Dalmatia (in modern Croatia) around 244 AD. His father was a former slave, and some sources say that Diocles was born into slavery himself. The first forty years of his life are mostly obscure, but he became a soldier and rose through the ranks to become a commander of Roman forces on the lower Danube.

His big break came in 282 AD when the Emperor Carus appointed him commander of the Protectores domestici, the élite cavalry force directly attached to the Imperial household, and conferred a consulship on him.

After the deaths of Carus and his son Numerian on campaign in Persia in 284, Diocles was unanimously chosen as emperor by the army. He Latinized his name to the more regal sounding Gaius Aurelius Valerius Diocletianus, and saw off a challenge to his title by Carus' other surviving son, the unpopular Carinus.

Diocletian's 21-year reign stabilized the Roman Empire after a period of anarchy which almost led to its collapse. He left imperial office in 305, the first Roman emperor to abdicate the position voluntarily. He lived out his retirement in his palace on the Dalmatian coast, tending to his vegetable gardens.

2. Justin I (450 – 527) – from swineherd to emperor

Justin was born in a small peasant village in what became modern Macedonia. He was employed as a swineherd until, as a teenager, a barbarian invasion forced him and two companions to flee. They arrived as refugees in the great city of Constantinople, capital of the Byzantine Empire, with nothing more than the ragged clothes on their backs and a sack of bread between them.

Justin joined the army as a palace guard for the Emperor Leo. Although Justin was illiterate, he shone as a natural military leader and rose rapidly through the ranks to become a general under the Emperor Anastasius I and commander of the palace guard.

It was an influential position which allowed him to secure election as emperor when the childless Anastasius died in 518. The 68-year-old Justin surrounded himself with trusted advisors – the most prominent being his nephew Flavius Petrus Sabbatius, whom he adopted as his son and invested with the name Justinian.

Justin's short reign was marked by strife within the Byzantine Empire and by 526 his health began to decline. He formally named Justinian as co-emperor, and was succeeded by him when he died the following year.

3. Theodora (500 – 548) – from prostitute to emprorer

Theodora's father was a bear trainer in Constantinople and her mother was a dancer and an actress. Employment as an actress at the time would include both "indecent exhibitions on stage" and providing sexual services off stage. Contemporary accounts relate that, from an early age, Theodora worked in a Constantinople brothel serving low-status customers and later performed on stage.

At the age of 16, she traveled to North Africa as the companion of a Syrian official. She stayed with him for almost four years, but he maltreated her and then abandoned her. She returned to Constantinople in 522 and gave up her former lifestyle, settling as a wool spinner in a house near the imperial palace.

Her beauty, wit, and charm drew the attention of Justinian, heir of the throne of his uncle, Emperor Justin I. Justinian pleaded with his uncle to repeal an old Roman law which prevented government officials from marrying actresses, and they married in 525. When Justin I died in 527, Justinian became emperor with Theodora his empress.

Theodora proved herself a worthy and able leader, particularly when riots broke out in Constantinople in 532. Unable to control the mob, Justinian and his officials prepared to flee. Theodora made an impassioned speech that they should stay and fight, and if necessary die in the 'royal purple', rather than live in disgrace as exiles. The rebellion was eventually crushed.

Following the revolt, Justinian and Theodora rebuilt and reformed Constantinople and made it the most splendid city the world had seen for centuries, building or rebuilding aqueducts, bridges, and more than twenty-five churches.

Theodora created her own centers of power and helped introduce many reforms in relation to women's rights. She had laws passed that prohibited forced prostitution, expanded the rights of women in divorce and property ownership, instituted the death penalty for rape, and forbade the killing of a wife who committed adultery.

The historian Procopius' Secret History presents a different view of Theodora. In her zeal to prevent forced prostitution she is said to have 'rounded up' 500 prostitutes, confining them to a convent. This, he narrates, even led to suicides as prostitutes sought to escape 'the unwelcome transformation.'

He also reports that Theodora was punctilious about court ceremony, making all senators, including patricians, prostrate themselves before the Imperial couple whenever they entered their presence. Government officials were treated like servants and reportedly had to show their respect to Theodora by lying face down and touching the instep of each of her feet with their lips.

Theodora died in 548 of what is thought to have been breast cancer. Justinian wept bitterly at her funeral.

4. Basil I (811 – 886) – from slave to emperor

Basil was born to peasant parents and spent part of his childhood in captivity in Bulgaria, where his family had, allegedly, been carried off as captives in 813. Basil lived there until 836, when he escaped to Byzantine-held territory in Thrace.

Basil entered service as a groom. While visiting the city of Patras with his master, he was fortunate to gain the favour of Danielis, a wealthy woman who took him into her household and endowed him with a fortune. He later came to the attention of the Byzantine emperor Michael III through his abilities as a horse tamer and in defeating a Bulgarian champion in a wrestling match. He soon became the emperor's companion, confidant, and bodyguard.

In 866 Basil convinced Michael III that his uncle Bardas coveted the Byzantine throne, and subsequently murdered Bardas with Michael's approval. Basil became the leading personality at court and was promoted as caesar, before being crowned co-emperor.

When Michael III started to favour another courtier, Basiliskianos, Basil organised the assassination of both men in 867. As an already acclaimed co-emperor, Basil automatically became the ruling emperor. There was little political reaction to the murder of Michael III due to his unpopularity with the bureaucrats of Constantinople and the Byzantine populace in general.

Basil reigned from 867 until his death in 886. Despite having no formal education and no military or administrative experience, he was perceived by the Byzantines as one of their greatest emperors. The Macedonian dynasty he founded ruled over what is regarded as the most glorious and prosperous era of the Byzantine Empire.

Basil died from a fever contracted after a serious hunting accident when his belt was caught in the antlers of a deer, and he was dragged for miles through the woods. He was saved by an attendant who cut him loose with a knife, but he suspected the attendant of trying to assassinate him and had the man executed shortly before he himself died.

5. Qutb al-din Aybak (1150 – 1210) – from slave to king

Qutb al-din Aibak. As a child Qutb was sold as a slave and raised at Nishapur (in modern day Iran). He eventually came into the possession of the Sultan of the Ghurid Empire, Muʿizz al-Dīn, who put him in charge of the royal stables.

Mu'izz had no offspring, but he treated his slaves as sons and trained them as soldiers and administrators; his most competent and loyal slaves rose to positions of importance in his army and government. Qutb was one such favourite. He was appointed to military command and rose through the ranks to become a general. After Muʿizz al-Dīn conquered Delhi in 1193, he left the consolidation of the Ghurid conquests in northwest India to Qutb.

When Muʿizz al-Dīn was assassinated in 1206, his Empire was divided amongst his leading slaves – with Qutb becoming the first Sultan of Delhi.

Qutb ruled for only four years. He died while playing polo in Lahore, when his horse fell, and he was impaled on the pommel of his saddle. However, he founded the Mamluk Dynasty which ruled the Delhi Sultanate until 1290 and conquered large areas of northern India.

6. Ivaylo of Bulgaria (died 1280) – from swineherd to emperor

Ivaylo of Bulgaria. Little is known of Ivaylo's early life other than he was from a peasant background and herded swine for payment. He was later nicknamed Bardokva ("radish" or "lettuce" in Bulgarian).

He rose to prominence in command of an army of discontented peasants which overthrew the forces of the Bulgarian emperor Constantine I. Ivaylo is credited with killing the emperor himself in battle in 1278.

He forced the Bulgarian nobles to accept him as emperor and consolidated his power by marrying Constantine's widow, the Empress Maria Kantakouzena.

To many the marriage was a disgrace. Maria was of noble birth, yet had married a swineherd, who had moreover killed her husband. Worse for Maria, Ivaylo proved to be abusive and was said to be physically beating her within a year of their marriage.

Ivaylo's reign was constantly challenged – externally by both the Byzantine Empire and the Mongol Empire, and internally by the Bulgarian nobility. He was eventually dethroned and forced into exile among the Mongols, who killed him in 1280.

Although his reign was short, his stunning rise to power has been used as an example of early, anti-feudal class warfare by Marxist historians. It also served as inspiration to Bulgarian freedom fighters during the Ottoman period of Bulgarian history.

7. Zhu Yuanzhang (1328 –1398) – from beggar to emperor

Zhu Yuanzhang was born into a desperately poor peasant farmer's family in Eastern China. When he was 16, a plague killed his entire family, except one of his brothers.

Destitute, Zhu Yuanzhang became a novice monk at a local Buddhist monastery, but was forced to leave when the monastery ran short of funds. For the next few years, he led the life of a wandering beggar, before returning to the monastery. He stayed until he was around 24 years old, and learned to read and write.

In 1352 the monastery was destroyed by the Mongol-ruled Yuan Dynasty army that was suppressing a local rebellion. Zhu joined one of the insurgent forces that had risen in rebellion and rose rapidly through the ranks to become a commander. As the rebel forces united, the ruthless and determined Zhu emerged as a leader and went on to overthrow the Yuan Dynasty and conquer the whole of China. Zhu proclaimed himself Emperor of China in 1368.

Titled the Hongwu Emperor, he reigned for 30 years until his death at the age of 69. He was the founder of the Ming Dynasty, which went on to rule China for 276 years and has been described as one of the greatest eras of orderly government and social stability in human history.

8. Karin Månsdotter (1550 – 1612) – from waitress to queen

Karin Månsdotter was born in Stockholm, Sweden to a soldier and later jailkeeper named Måns. Her mother sold vegetables on the city square.

Both her parents are believed to have died around 1560 and Karin went into service in the household of royal court musician Gert Cantor. Part of his house was a tavern and it is likely that Karin came to the attention of King Eric XIV of Sweden in 1564 when she served him as a waitress. A year later she had become his mistress.

Eric had maintained numerous mistresses up to this point, but when Karin entered his life, he dismissed them all. She was given expensive clothes, her own apartment and servants, and appeared with the king openly at court. She also received an education and learned to read and write. When she gave birth to a daughter in 1566 and a son in

1568, the children were treated as legitimate princess and prince.

Karin was described as very beautiful with long blond hair, and her personality seems to have been calm, humble and natural. The king was mentally unstable, and she seems to have been the only one who could calm him down – which at first made her useful to the nobles at court.

However, while she had no personal enemies, she was not respected, and their official marriage in 1568 was considered a scandal at court. It was followed by Karin's coronation as queen, which was celebrated with great festivities in Stockholm to legitimize her status as queen. Karin's peasant relatives were present, dressed in clothes made for them by the royal tailor.

Soon after the coronation, King Eric's brothers rebelled against him and had the royal couple imprisoned – their children being placed in the care of the Dowager Queen. Karin gave birth to two children in captivity in 1570 and 1572, both of whom died in prison, so she was separated from her husband to prevent the birth of any more legitimate offspring.

Queen Karin and her children were taken to Finland where she remained under house arrest until the death of her husband in 1577. She was treated with kindness in Finland and given the royal estate Liuksiala Manor, where she lived the rest of her life until her death in 1612.

9. Catherine I of Russia (1684 – 1727) – from washerwoman to empress

Catherine I of Russia was born in 1684 as Marta Skowrońska, daughter of a Lithuanian peasant. Her parents died of the plague around 1689 and Marta was sent by an aunt to Marienburg (in modern Latvia) where she was raised by a Lutheran pastor, serving in his household as a lowly scullery maid or washerwoman. She was not taught to read or write and remained illiterate throughout her life.

When Russian forces captured Marienburg in 1702, Marta was supposedly sent to work in the laundry of the victorious regiment and later travelled back to Russia with them.

Afterwards she became part of the household of Prince Alexander Menshikov, who was the best friend of the Tsar of Russia, Peter the Great. In 1703, while visiting Menshikov at home, Peter first saw Marta, who was considered a very beautiful young woman, as well as compassionate, charming and always cheerful. Within a year, she was well established in the Tsar's household as his mistress, and gave birth to a son. She went on to bear him a total of twelve children, but only two of them whom survived into adulthood.

Marta took the name Catherine Alexeyevna and married Peter in St. Petersburg in 1712, becoming the Tsarina. When Peter elevated the Russian Tsardom to Empire, she became Empress and was later officially crowned and named co-ruler.

When Peter died in 1725 without naming a successor, Catherine was popularly proclaimed as the first woman to rule Imperial Russia in her own right. She died after only 16-months on the throne, but was able to reduce the size of the empire's bloated military to relieve the tax burden on the peasantry.

10. Henri Christophe (1767 – 1820) – from slave to king

Henri Christophe was born, probably in Grenada, the son of a slave mother and a freeman. He was brought to Haiti as a slave.

In 1779 he is thought to have served as a drummer boy with French forces at the Siege of Savannah, a battle during the American Revolutionary War. When he was sent back to Haiti he worked as a domestic servant in a hotel in Cap-Français, the first capital of the French colony of Saint-Domingue. Most of his pay went to his master. Skilled at dealing with the wealthy white French planters, he worked his way up to manage the hotel restaurant. This enabled him to eventually buy his freedom from slavery.

From 1791 Christophe distinguished himself as a soldier in the Haïtian Revolution, a slave revolt in Saint-Domingue which eventually led to the founding of the Republic of Haiti. He quickly rose to become an officer and fought for years under the revolutionary leader Toussaint Louverture, helping to defeat the French colonists, the Spanish, British, and finally French national troops. By 1802 Louverture had promoted Christophe to general.

After Louverture's death, there was a power struggle for control of the island. Christophe set up his own domain in northern Haiti, which he ruled as King Henry I from 1811.

King Henry was an unpopular, autocratic monarch. To ensure the recovery of Haiti's war-torn agricultural production on the plantations, he introduced a system of enforced labour in lieu of taxes, which was little different to the slavery that Haiti had struggled to overthrow. He also began massive building projects, including eight palaces and six châteaus for his own use, as well as creating an elaborate system of Haïtian nobility that was widely mocked outside of his realm.

Towards the end of his reign, King Henry became increasingly ill and, with public sentiment against his vision of a feudal society, he committed suicide by shooting himself with a silver bullet rather than risk a coup and assassination. His son and heir was assassinated 10 days later and his kingdom became part of the Haitian republic in 1821.

In these examples we understand that exceptional people were able to take advantage of extraordinary circumstances and utilize their individual talents or characteristics to rise above the position the collective or society had designated as their rightful position. This was certainly the exception as opposed to the rule. These people lived in societies that frowned upon individualism and even punished those who elected not to conform to their pre-destined position by demotions, imprisonment, beatings, or death.

To see individuals rise above their status at birth was far more common in the English colonies of North America, later to become the United States of America. In the United States, to rise above an individual's birth status became the rule and not the exception. Some examples would be Alexander Hamilton, Andrew Jackson, Calvin Coolidge, and Harry Truman. In the business world examples would be Andrew Carnegie, John D Rockefeller, and Henry Ford.

The list goes on and on. The list could include relatives of yours, perhaps your grandparents who immigrated legally through Ellis Island after leaving the oppressive state of some collectivist European nation. After struggling to free themselves from the entangling red tape of the controlling big government of any collectivist state, these brave pioneers endured many hardships to witness Lady Liberty in New York Harbor. They then did what Americans do; they put forth a dedicated effort to provide for their families, so their children could achieve more than they did.

Most recently we have seen legal immigrants from Asia; places like Viet Nam, Thailand, and the Philippines, also fleeing from oppressive collectivist government to live in "the land of the free." These people also overcame many hardships, and now appreciate the opportunity inherent within individualism.

This is how Wikipedia reports on the following:

Alexander Hamilton (January 11, 1755 or 1757 – July 12, 1804) was an American statesman and one of the Founding Fathers of the United States. He was an influential interpreter and promoter of the U.S. Constitution, as well as the founder of the nation's financial system, the Federalist Party, the United States Coast Guard, and The New York Post newspaper. As the first Secretary of the Treasury, Hamilton was the main author of the economic policies of the George Washington administration. He took the lead in the funding of the states' debts by the Federal government, as well as the establishment of a national bank, a system of tariffs, and friendly trade relations with Britain. His vision included a strong central government led by a vigorous executive branch, a strong commercial economy, with a national bank and support for manufacturing, plus a strong military

Hamilton was born out of wedlock in Charlestown, Nevis. His Scottish-born father, James A. Hamilton, was the fourth son of Alexander Hamilton, laird of Grange, Ayrshire. His mother, born Rachel Faucette, was half-British and half-French Huguenot. Orphaned as a child by his mother's death and his father's abandonment, Hamilton was taken in by an older cousin and later by a prosperous merchant family. He was recognized for his intelligence and talent, and sponsored by a group of wealthy local men to travel to New York City to pursue his education. Hamilton attended King's College (now Columbia University), choosing to stay in the Thirteen Colonies to seek his fortune.

Andrew Jackson (March 15, 1767 – June 8, 1845) was an American soldier and statesman who served as the seventh President of the United States from 1829 to 1837. Before being elected to the presidency, Jackson gained fame as a general in the United States Army and served in both houses of Congress. As president, Jackson sought to advance the rights of the "common man" against a "corrupt aristocracy" and to preserve the Union.

Andrew Jackson was born in the Waxhaws region of the Carolinas. His parents were Scots-Irish colonists Andrew and Elizabeth Hutchinson Jackson, Presbyterians who had emigrated from present day Northern Ireland two years earlier. Jackson's father was born in Carrickfergus, County Antrim, in current-day Northern Ireland, around 1738 Jackson's parents lived in the village of Boneybefore, also in County Antrim. Jackson's exact birthplace is unclear because he was born about the time his mother was making a difficult trip home from burying Jackson's father. The area was so remote that the border between North and South Carolina had not been officially surveyed.

John Calvin Coolidge Jr. (July 4, 1872 – January 5, 1933) was the 30th President of the United States (1923–29). A Republican lawyer from Vermont, Coolidge worked his way up the ladder of Massachusetts state politics, eventually becoming governor of that state. His response to the Boston Police Strike of 1919 thrust him into the national spotlight and gave him a reputation as a man of decisive action. Soon after, he was elected as the 29th vice president in 1920 and succeeded to the presidency upon the sudden death of Warren G. Harding in 1923. Elected in his own right in 1924, he gained a reputation as a small-government conservative, and as a man who said very little, although having a rather dry sense of humor.

John Calvin Coolidge Jr. was born in Plymouth Notch, Windsor County, Vermont, on July 4, 1872, the only U.S. president to be born on Independence Day. He was the elder of the two children of John Calvin Coolidge Sr. (1845–1926) and Victoria Josephine Moor (1846–85). Coolidge Senior engaged in many occupations, including farmer, storekeeper and public servant.

Harry S. Truman (May 8, 1884 – December 26, 1972) was an American statesman who served as the 33rd President of the United States (1945–53), taking the office upon the death of Franklin D. Roosevelt. A World War I veteran, he assumed the presidency during the waning months of World War II and the beginning of the Cold War. He is known for approving the atomic bombings of Hiroshima and Nagasaki and the Marshall Plan to rebuild the economy of Western Europe, the establishment of the Truman Doctrine and NATO against Soviet and Chinese communism, and for intervening in the Korean War.

Harry S. Truman was born in Lamar, Missouri on May 8, 1884, the oldest child of John Anderson Truman (1851–1914) and Martha Ellen Young Truman (1852–1947). John Truman was a farmer and livestock dealer. The family lived in Lamar until Harry was ten months old, when they moved to a farm near Harrisonville, Missouri. The family next moved to Belton, and in 1887 to his grandparents' 600-acre farm in Grandview. When Truman was six, his parents moved to Independence, so he could attend the Presbyterian Church Sunday School. Truman did not attend a traditional school until he was eight.

Andrew Carnegie (November 25, 1835 – August 11, 1919) was a Scottish-American industrialist. Carnegie led the expansion of the American steel industry in the late 19th century and is often identified as one of the richest people (and richest Americans) ever. He became a leading philanthropist in the United States, and in the British Empire. During the last 18 years of his life, he gave away about $350 million to charities, foundations, and universities—almost 90 percent of his fortune. His 1889 article proclaiming, "The Gospel of Wealth" called on the rich to use their wealth to improve society, and stimulated a wave of philanthropy.

Carnegie was born in Dunfermline, Scotland, and immigrated to the United States with his parents in 1848. Carnegie started work as a telegrapher, and by the 1860s had investments in railroads, railroad sleeping cars, bridges, and oil derricks. He accumulated further wealth as a bond salesman, raising money for American enterprise in Europe. He built Pittsburgh's Carnegie Steel Company, which he sold to J.P. Morgan in 1901 for $480 million. It became the U.S. Steel Corporation. After selling Carnegie Steel, he surpassed

John D. Rockefeller as the richest American for the next couple of years.

John D Rockefeller Sr. (July 8, 1839 – May 23, 1937) was an American oil industry business magnate and philanthropist. He is widely considered the wealthiest American of all time, and the richest person in modern history.

Rockefeller was born into a large family in upstate New York and was shaped by his con man father and religious mother. His family moved several times before eventually settling in Cleveland, Ohio. Rockefeller became an assistant bookkeeper at the age of 16, and went into a business partnership with Maurice B. Clark and his brothers at 20. After buying them out, he and his brother William founded Rockefeller & Andrews with Samuel Andrews. Instead of drilling for oil, he concentrated on refining.

Henry Ford (July 30, 1863 – April 7, 1947) was an American captain of industry and a business magnate, the founder of the Ford Motor Company, and the sponsor of the development of the assembly line technique of mass production. Although Ford did not invent the automobile or the assembly line. He developed and manufactured the first automobile that many middle-class Americans could afford. In doing so, Ford converted the automobile from an expensive curiosity into a practical conveyance that would profoundly impact the landscape of the 20th Century.

Henry Ford was born on a farm in Greenfield Township, Michigan. His father, William Ford (1826–1905), was born in County Cork, Ireland, to a family that was originally from Somerset, England, His mother, Mary Ford 1839–1876), was born in Michigan as the youngest child of Belgian immigrants; her parents died when she was a child and she was adopted by neighbors, the O'Herns.

Many of the stories of other brave legal immigrants would read like those above. Although their stories might not be published, their children and grandchildren know the stories and share the pride in this unique country their parents and grandparents held. In many of these individuals, the gratitude for the freedom, liberty, and opportunity provided under individualism is also greatly appreciated by these true Americans.

Our Founders in the Declaration of Independence said:

"When in the Course of human events it becomes necessary for one people to dissolve the political bands which have connected them with another and to assume among the powers of the earth, the separate and equal station to which the Laws of Nature and of Nature's God entitle them, a decent respect to the opinions of mankind requires that they should declare the causes which impel them to the separation.

We hold these truths to be self-evident, that all men are created equal, that they are endowed by their Creator with certain unalienable Rights, that among these are Life, Liberty and the pursuit of Happiness. — That to secure these rights, Governments are instituted among Men, deriving their just powers from the consent of the governed, — That whenever any Form of Government becomes destructive of these ends, it is the Right of the People to alter or to abolish it, and to institute new Government, laying its foundation on such principles and organizing its powers in such form, as to them shall seem most likely to effect their Safety and Happiness."

The Founders were abundantly clear that individualism is a right granted by the Creator and it is not the right of man or government to control or alter. It is the Creator who granted the unalienable rights of, amongst others, Life, Liberty, and the Pursuit of Happiness. Our right to Liberty is not to be dictated by some man imposed condition.

So, what Is Liberty? (2)

Here is a precise definition for freedom/liberty:

A condition in which a man's will regarding his own person and property is unopposed by any other will.

That is the bedrock. From there you can add other aspects if you wish, but you cannot deviate from this core and still be talking about "liberty."

For example, Thomas Jefferson used the same core idea (notice the inclusion of "will"), but added a political aspect:

Rightful liberty is unobstructed action according to our will within limits drawn around us by the equal rights of others. I do not add "within the limits of the law" because law is often but the tyrant's will, and always so when it violates the rights of the individual.

The great John Locke also held to this core, but took it in a more philosophical direction:

All men are naturally in a state of perfect freedom to order their actions, and dispose of their possessions and persons as they think fit, within the bounds of the law of Nature, without asking leave or depending upon the will of any other man.

Personally, I like a very plain version of the same sentiments:

We should be allowed to do whatever we want, so long as we don't hurt others.

Individualism thus became the core of a free society which proclaims liberty for all. We cannot be free unless we as individuals are able to have our own thoughts, make our own decisions, and live our lives independent of government dictates, so long as we do not harm others.

A critical part of freedom and liberty is that we as an individual are also able to pursue our own happiness. Our place in life is not to be determined by societal or governmental dictates. Our right to pursue our own happiness should have nothing to do with what others have dictated since this right, along with Life, and Liberty, is an unalienable right given by our Creator. We in a free society, are not only able to, but are encouraged to, rise to the full potential of the gifts given to us by our Creator. In a free society that values liberty, individuals who apply these gifts should not be admonished or punished for their efforts or achievement. As individuals, we must also recognize and be willing to accept the consequences, good or bad, for our decisions made and actions taken as individuals. We, as individuals, cannot exercise the mentality that would blame our failures on society or others. Our decisions are our responsibility.

We should be teaching children that their talents and efforts are valued and cherished. When a child excels in a sport, for whatever reason; ability, effort, or both, they should be recognized for that achievement and not receive the same recognition given to a child for participating. When a child excels in the classroom, for whatever reason; ability, effort, or both, they should be recognized for that achievement and not receive the same recognition given to a child for participating. When a child excels musically, for whatever reason; ability, effort, or both, they should be recognized for that achievement and not receive the same recognition given to a child for participating.

Economic individualism's basic premise is that the pursuit of self-interest and the right to own private property are morally defensible and legally legitimate. Its major corollary is that the state exists to protect individual rights. Subject to certain restrictions, individuals (alone or with others) are free to decide where to invest, what to produce or sell, and what prices to charge. There is no natural limit to the range of their efforts in terms of assets, sales, and profits; or the number of customers, employees, and investors; or whether they operate in local, regional, national, or international markets. (3)

This is the essence of freedom and liberty. This is the essence of a free enterprise system. This is the essence of the Creator granted unalienable right; Pursuit of Happiness. A free enterprise system, or what we commonly refer to as a capitalistic economic system, can only exist and flourish in a society based on individualism. It is the individual entrepreneur, investor, or worker (sometimes all three in one) that makes the decisions. It is the individual that reaps the rewards or suffers bad consequences because of their decisions. It is the individual who is responsible for those consequences. When society or government assumes responsibility for results through a punitive tax system or punitive regulatory system, or assumes responsibility through a welfare system, a government bailout system, or special grants or favors, a free enterprise system based on individualism no longer exists.

The concept of individualism is rooted in historical contexts where people's personal differences were dismissed or even punished by the ruling body. The United States is known for having a strong bent towards individualism because it was founded by people who sought the freedom to practice whatever religion they chose, to be able to think and speak freely and openly, to be able to make decisions without government interference, and to pursue their own happiness reaping the rewards (monetary or other) or be responsible for any negative results. The counterpoints to individualism are socialism and communism (among others). Those who prefer individualism often site fear of governmental control over their life decisions as the reason for that inclination. We will explore the alternatives in later chapters.

(1) by Josie Webster for History - Ancient, Medieval & Modern
(2) What is Liberty Exactly? FREEMANSPERSPECTIVE · May 28th, 2013
(3) Capitalism by Robert Hessen

Chapter 2. TYRANNY OR FREEDOM

Collectivism is a political theory associated with communism, socialism, progressivism, and modern-day liberalism. More broadly, it is the idea that people should prioritize the good of society over the welfare of the individual. Collectivism has to do with political theories that put the collective before the individual. Collectivism is the opposite of individualism.

Collectivism means the subjugation of the individual to a collective—whether to a race, class, or state; it does not matter. Collectivism holds that man must be chained to collective action and collective thought for the sake of what is called "the common good." Just as individualism is mandatory for the existence of a free society, collectivism is essential for a totalitarian state.

Ayn Rand described collectivism this way: "Collectivism holds that the individual has no rights, that his life and work belong to the group (to "society," to the tribe, the state, the nation) and that the group may sacrifice him at its own whim to its own interests. The only way to implement a doctrine of that kind is by means of brute force -- and statism has always been the political corollary of collectivism."

Under collectivism, the individual has no right other than those granted by the state for the period of time the state determines to grant those rights. This is in direct contrast to the American principles per the "Declaration of

Independence" where the American founders said, "all men are created equal, that they are endowed by their Creator with certain unalienable Rights, that among these are Life, Liberty and the pursuit of Happiness. That to secure these rights, Governments are instituted among Men, deriving their just powers from the consent of the governed."

According to the founders, our rights are not for the state to give but they were given to us by the Creator. Therefore, our founders disagreed with the collectivist who claims that all rights are determined by the state or man and controlled by the state or man. The founders went on to argue that not only are the rights of mankind given by the Creator and not in any way under the purview of man or the state, but that the state has no rights, other than those, we the people give the state. Individualism and collectivism are the exact opposites.

Collectivism is the idea that the individual's life belongs not to him but to the collective or society of which he is merely a part, that he has no rights, and that he must sacrifice his values and goals for the collective's "greater good." According to collectivism, the collective or society is the basic unit of moral concern, and the individual is of value only insofar as he serves the collective. As one advocate of this idea puts it: "Man has no rights except those which society permits him to enjoy. From the day of his birth until the day of his death, society allows him to enjoy certain so-called rights and deprives him of others; not . . . because society desires especially to favor or oppress the individual, but because its own preservation, welfare, and happiness are the prime considerations." (1)

Collectivism is therefore essential to a totalitarian state and individualism is essential to a free society. In a collectivist society, children are taught that they are not valued as individuals for their talents and efforts, but are rewarded the same as any other participant regardless of their individual ability and effort. The children are taught they will be rewarded the same if their performance and effort is exemplary as they would be rewarded if their performance and effort is poor or unworthy. Thus, all children receive the same trophy and no child is recognized for outstanding academic achievement, for instance. In the collectivist society, the reasoning would be that recognition of an individual for exemplary achievement and effort could damage the collective as a whole and this would be detrimental to the collective.

The same reasoning that applies to rights under individualism and collectivism also applies to economic systems. In a collectivist society, it is considered that everything belongs to the state and it is up to the state to distribute economic benefits as the state determines to be in the best interest of the state. The collectivist would say that the income an individual earns is not the property of the individual because it is the state who made it possible for the individual to earn the income by providing a means for jobs to exist. Therefore, the collectivist says, the state can and should determine how much of the income the individual is paid, the individual can keep. In addition, the collectivist says, it is only fair that a steeply progressive income tax be implemented because it was the state who enabled certain individuals to earn higher incomes than others. It is only fair that those who benefited more from the state's efforts, contribute to the overall welfare of the state in a greater proportionate share.

The collectivist also believes that a steeply progressive death tax or estate tax be invoked. Remember, everything ultimately belongs to the state, therefore at death, the collectivist says, it is only fair and right that the assets an individual was allowed to accumulate during his lifetime should be returned to the state, the rightful owner. The collectivist believes that the good of the collective or the state should be placed before the rights of the heirs of the individual. After all, these assets of the deceased, can be and will be more beneficial when returned to the state, the rightful owner, so the assets can be redistributed in a manner that benefits the collective as opposed those assets benefiting the individual heirs of the deceased.

A centrally planned economy, as opposed to a free enterprise economy, is in the best interest of the collective, so believes the collectivist. A free enterprise economy produces goods and services that are demanded by the public. This demand is based on the total dollars individuals are willing to allocate to different products and services. The collectivist argues that the free enterprise system produces goods and services demanded by a small segment of the collective and does not necessarily produce the goods and services that would be in the best interest of the collective.

In a centrally planned economy, the goods and services to be produced will and should be determined by a group of central planners who will dictate that the goods and services produced are for the good of the collective and not a few of the financial elite. The central planners, it is believed by the collectivist, are more capable of determining short term and long-term needs of the collective than would the individual producers of goods or providers of services. The individual producers of goods or providers of services will allocate their resources to the product or service that will provide them the greatest benefit and will not consider what is in the best interest of the collective.

By definition, a centrally planned economy is an economic system where the government makes decisions for the economy, instead of those decisions being made due to the interacting between businesses and consumers. Unlike a market economy, where business owners and private citizens can make production decisions, this form of economy controls the production and distribution of products, as well as the use of resources. Also, enterprises that are owned by the state undertake the production of goods and services.

List of perceived Advantages of Centrally Planned Economy:

1. It promotes equality among consumers.

Since the government controls all aspects of production, there will be no chance of monopoly to occur, which means that the gap between the rich and the poor will be reduced, as all government policies will be designed to bring about social and economic equality.

2. It allows the government to monitor all aspects of economy.

In a centrally planned economy, the government will be able to keep proper tabs on the supply, demand, prices, and other aspects surrounding goods and services. It can also indirectly keep a watch on any signs of inflation that might occur.

3. It does not hinder economic projects to be carried out immediately.

There will be no need to wait for private investments for specific projects to get underway, unlike in other economic systems, such as capitalism. Here, the government reigns supreme, which means that it can start and end a project that the country might require, such as infrastructures, health facilities, and sanitation services. (2)

You will notice in the first perceived benefit it states, "Since the government controls all aspects of production." This assumption is critical, not only to a centrally planned economy, but to a collectivist state. The control of all aspects of production can be maintained in different ways.

In the Marxist societies, all means of production were owned by the state. No individual was allowed to own the means of production, be it a factory or land. Lenin, in the early days of the Soviet Union, confiscated all the crops grown by the peasants on what was government owned land. Production quickly decreased, and Lenin witnessed widespread starvation among the Russian people. Trotsky convinced Lenin to allow the peasant to keep a portion of his production, and amazingly production increased. Under either of these scenarios, central planning was still imposed.

In Germany, when it was controlled by the National Socialist German Workers Party, the government did not own the factories and farmland. Private individuals owned the means of production. Nevertheless, Germany's economy was a centrally planned economy. Even though ownership remained with the individuals, the German government monitored all aspects of the economy including dictating what was to be produced and in what amounts. Demands for goods by individual consumers were not considered as the government determined what was in the best interest of the collective. Yes, the wishes or needs of the collective or state determined production.

In most economies today, we see central planned economies that are euphemistically called free enterprise economies. The governments centrally plan the economies of the individual countries with regulation and tax incentives or punishments. In addition, governments are picking winners and losers, demanding certain types of production, and demanding certain types of services by giving grants and subsidies. Grants and subsidies, as a part of these centrally planned economies, have been prevalent in the energy industry, the health industry, the financial industry, and the transportation industry as examples.

The collectivist believes that it is always in the best interest of the group to have a centrally planned economy so the good of the collective is served. They believe that by implementing a centrally planned economy the greater good will be served because the central planners are able to curtail income "inequalities," promote social justice, and produce products and services that the collective needs and is best for them as opposed to what individuals desire.

All that the collectivist advocates and proclaims is best for their respective nation and society as a whole, is the antithesis of what the founders said was necessary for a free nation to exist. The founders said rights are not for the state to give and thus the state cannot take away the individuals rights. Even if the collectivist determines that the exercise of certain speech is not in the best interest of the collective, the founders said the individual still had the right to speak. Even if the collectivist determines that the exercise of a certain set of religious beliefs were not in the best interest of the collective, the founders said the collective could not abridge the exercise by the individual of those religious beliefs. Even if the collectivist determined that the peaceful assembly of a group of individuals was not in their best interest, the founders said they still had the right to assemble. Even if the collectivist determined that the goals, desires, and wishes of an individual performed in his pursuit of happiness was not in the best interest of the collective because it somehow harmed the self-image of others, the founders said the individual still had the right to pursue their happiness.

The founders said the rights of the individuals could not be taken or abridged, even if the exercise of those rights was determined not to be in the best interest of the collective. The founders said the rights of the individual were not to be subjugated to the perceived good of the collective. The founders believed in the goodness of individualism and the evil of collectivism. The "Declaration of Independence" and the "United States Constitution" are not compatible with a collectivist society. The collectivist understands that the "Declaration of Independence" and the "United States Constitution" must be neutralized or outright obliterated to bring about the collectivist desired society.

(1) A. Maurice Low, "What is Socialism? III: An Explanation of 'The Rights' Men Enjoy in a State of Civilized Society," The North American Review, vol. 197, no. 688 (March 1913), p. 406.

(2) Contact US, The Global Issues Blog.

Chapter 3. PLANNED TRANSFORMATION

It is the goal of the collectivist to revolutionize the world so that all people are under the same collectivist system where all are under a system of centralized social and economic control, and where the perceived good of society or the collective is always the priority over the welfare of the individual. In this system the goals, desires, and ambitions of the individual are secondary to what is thought to be in the best interest of the collective as defined by the Dictatorship of the Proletariat per Karl Marx.

Marx called for revolution by the worker or the proletariat over the capitalist or bourgeoisie so there would then be only one class, or as he said a classless society. In this classless society, all individuals would be secondary to the collective. Communism or Marxism is the highest form of collectivism.

Marx wrote in The German Ideology:

"Communism can only be effected through a union, which by the character of the proletariat itself can again only be a universal one, and through a revolution, in which, on the one hand, the power of the earlier mode of production and intercourse and social organization is overthrown, and, on the other hand, there develops the universal character and the energy of the proletariat, without which the revolution cannot be accomplished; and in which, further, the proletariat rids itself of everything that still clings to it from its previous position in society."

It should go without saying that this is not just a view of "social change," but that it is mechanical or predestined. Struggle is at the heart of Marx and Engels' theory of working-class revolution, which is why they ended the Communist Manifesto with this call to action:

"The Communists disdain to conceal their views and aims. They openly declare that their ends can be attained only by the forcible overthrow of all existing social conditions. Let the ruling classes tremble at a Communistic revolution. The proletarians have nothing to lose but their chains. They have a world to win."

Marx and Engels understood that revolution per se might not be the means to collectivism or communism in all situations, as they noted in other writings, but when not revolution then their collectivist society would have to come about through a form of transformation. Frederick Engels, in 1847 wrote "The Principles of Communism." The following is an excerpt detailing different means by which this transformation could be implemented and accomplished. Much of this became a part of the "Communist Manifesto". As you read through the different policies that Engels details for the transformation, notice how many have already been adopted in the United States.

"Above all, it will establish a democratic constitution, and through this, the direct or indirect dominance of the proletariat. Direct in England, where the proletarians are already a majority of the people.

Indirect in France and Germany, where the majority of the people consists not only of proletarians, but also of small peasants and petty bourgeois who are in the process of falling into the proletariat, who are more and more dependent in all their political interests on the proletariat, and who must, therefore, soon adapt to the demands of the proletariat. Perhaps this will cost a second struggle, but the outcome can only be the victory of the proletariat.

Democracy would be wholly valueless to the proletariat if it were not immediately used as a means for putting through measures directed against private property and ensuring the livelihood of the proletariat. The main measures, emerging as the necessary result of existing relations, are the following:

(i) Limitation of private property through progressive taxation, heavy inheritance taxes, abolition of inheritance through collateral lines (brothers, nephews, etc.) forced loans, etc.

(ii) Gradual expropriation of landowners, industrialists, railroad magnates and shipowners, partly through competition by state industry, partly directly through compensation in the form of bonds.

(iii) Confiscation of the possessions of all emigrants and rebels against the majority of the people.

(iv) Organization of labor or employment of proletarians on publicly owned land, in factories and workshops, with competition among the workers being abolished and with the factory owners, in so far as they still exist, being obliged to pay the same high wages as those paid by the state.

(v) An equal obligation on all members of society to work until such time as private property has been completely abolished. Formation of industrial armies, especially for agriculture.

(vi) Centralization of money and credit in the hands of the state through a national bank with state capital, and the suppression of all private banks and bankers.

(vii) Increase in the number of national factories, workshops, railroads, ships; bringing new lands into cultivation and improvement of land already under cultivation – all in proportion to the growth of the capital and labor force at the disposal of the nation.

(viii) Education of all children, from the moment they can leave their mother's care, in national establishments at national cost. Education and production together.

(ix) Construction, on public lands, of great palaces as communal dwellings for associated groups of citizens engaged in both industry and agriculture and combining in their way of life the advantages of urban and rural conditions while avoiding the one-sidedness and drawbacks of each.

(x) Destruction of all unhealthy and jerry-built dwellings in urban districts.

(xi) Equal inheritance rights for children born in and out of wedlock.

(xii) Concentration of all means of transportation in the hands of the nation.

It is impossible, of course, to carry out all these measures at once. But one will always bring others in its wake. Once the first radical attack on private property has been launched, the proletariat will find itself forced to go ever further, to concentrate increasingly in the hands of the state all capital, all agriculture, all transport, all trade. All the foregoing measures are directed to this end; and they will become practicable and feasible, capable of producing their centralizing effects to precisely the degree that the proletariat, through its labor, multiplies the country's productive forces.

Finally, when all capital, all production, all exchange has been brought together in the hands of the nation, private property will disappear of its own accord, money will become superfluous, and production will so expand, and man so change that society will be able to slough off whatever of its old economic habits may remain."

During the years Lenin and other communists were exiled from Russia, they learned what became their trademark and has since become the trademark of all collectivists in the implementing of their agenda; lying, cheating, counterfeiting, using aliases and other forms of trickery and deceit. Lenin, and other Bolsheviks were surprised during

World War I that workers were willing to fight for their respective nations against other workers as opposed to rising united against the capitalists to throw of their chains of bondage. In order to overcome this, Lenin and the Bolsheviks learned to use various covert tactics to manipulate the workers into action. Communist agents secretly infiltrated unions and steered the agendas of these unions in the Bolshevik direction. This tactic worked so well that secret Bolshevik agents were also placed in the media, in entertainment, and in academia.

Although we do not have recorded audio of an early meeting of the Communist International or the COMM intern, we do know based on history the thrust of the conversation. Lenin was leading a discussion on how their propaganda effort could become more affective in the West, particularly the United States. The Communists were well aware, especially at the end of the First World War, that Americans were steeped in patriotism, individualism, and in the belief of American exceptionalism.

What we know came from that meeting was that the Bolsheviks would use the same tactics on the West, primarily the United States, that they had used in Russia to bring about and secure their revolution. Those tactics would be, lying, cheating, counterfeiting, using aliases and other forms of trickery and deceit as they infiltrated, penetrated, and controlled the channels they knew they could use to indoctrinate the Americans in collectivism. These channels would again be the same channels they infiltrated in Russia to win the revolution; the school systems or academia, the daily press or the media, and the centers of entertainment or what is referred to as Hollywood.

One of the successes the COMM intern had in their quest to influence American academia was the hold they had on George Counts. Wikipedia says "George Sylvester Counts (December 9, 1889 – November 10, 1974) was an American educator and influential education theorist. An early proponent of the progressive education movement of John Dewey, Counts became its leading critic affiliated with the school of Social reconstructionism in education. Counts is credited for influencing several subsequent theories, particularly critical pedagogy. Counts wrote dozens of important papers and 29 books about education. He was also highly active in politics as a leading advocate of teachers' unions, the head of the American Federation of Teachers, the founder of the New York State Liberal Party, and as a candidate for the U.S. Senate."

What else we know about Counts was that he was a professor of Education at Columbia University's Teacher College from 1927 until his retirement. Counts was selected to travel to Russia to learn about Russia and the Bolsheviks by the Teacher College. While in Russia, the KGB, not necessarily known to Counts, selected a Russian graduate student, Anna Perlmutter, to handle Counts. She became his administrative assistant and worked for him through his career at Columbia.

Counts claimed he had translated a Russian book on education called "New Russia's Primer." Maybe he did or maybe Anna did, but regardless it was introduced as a guide into American education as it screamed, "Capitalism is corrupt! Russia's experiment is working." The book was a Russian internal propaganda training book. It was designed by the Soviets to introduce their school children to the ways of Communism and the communist five-year plan. It was well developed and indoctrinated the Russian children at an early age. It also, thanks to Counts, paved the way for American children to be indoctrinated in collectivism, namely communism, as well.

Wikipedia description of Walter Duranty reads like this: "Walter Duranty (May 25, 1884 – October 3, 1957) was a Liverpool-born, Anglo-American journalist who served as the Moscow Bureau Chief of The New York Times for fourteen years (1922–1936) following the Bolshevik victory in the Russian Civil War (1918–1921).

In 1932, Duranty received a Pulitzer Prize for a series of reports about the Soviet Union, 11 of them published in June 1931. He was criticized for his subsequent denial of widespread famine (1932–33) in the USSR, most particularly the mass starvation in Ukraine. Years later, there were calls to revoke his Pulitzer; The New York Times, which submitted his works for the prize in 1932, wrote that his later articles denying the famine constituted "some of the worst reporting to appear in this newspaper."

Duranty arrived in Russia around the end of 1921 or very early 1922, and like Counts had very little Russian knowledge. In the defense of both Counts and Duranty, there really were not many people that had much knowledge of the new Russia. And like Counts, this made Duranty an inviting target for the COMM intern and their plan to infiltrate the American media. Duranty gave the KGB a direct link to the American public through the New York Times.

While in Russia, Duranty had constant and close contact with Konstantin Umansky who worked for the Soviet press bureau and later for the Soviet press agency TASS. He eventually worked for the Soviet Ministry of Foreign Affairs and became ambassador to the United States and then to Mexico. This type of career trajectory would seem to indicate that he was a KGB officer, even during the time he had close contact with Duranty when Duranty had to report to Umansky each time he filed a story.

Duranty was granted an interview with Stalin in 1930. He also wrote a glowing review on Stalin's results of collectivizing agriculture in the Soviet Union that in fact resulted in famine in the Ukraine. Duranty ignored the truth and reported that there was no actual starvation, but people were dying because of diseases.

When Franklin Roosevelt announced that the United States would officially recognize the Soviet Union, Duranty accompanied the Russian Minister of Foreign Affairs to Washington DC. This was the reward the Soviets and

Franklin Roosevelt gave to Duranty for spinning the Soviet point of view for the last 12 years. When Duranty returned to Russia he was rewarded with another interview with Stalin in the Kremlin. According to Duranty, Stalin told him, "you bet on our horse to win when others thought it had no chance and I am sure that have you have not lost by it." Duranty repeated this quote with great pride for the rest of his life.

Duranty reported favorably on the Soviet Union through the New York times for those years and he became recognized as an expert on the Soviet Union. Many of his reports, of course including his spin on the Ukraine famine, have been shown to be false. His favorable Soviet spinning did allow him to live the good life while living in Moscow. His pro Soviet reporting through the New York Times set a tone at the Times that has not changed to this day.

Wikipedia's description of Dorothy Parker reads like this: "Dorothy Parker (August 22, 1893 – June 7, 1967) was an American poet, short story writer, critic, and satirist, best known for her wit, wisecracks and eye for 20th-century urban foibles."

From a conflicted and unhappy childhood, Parker rose to acclaim, both for her literary output in publications such as The New Yorker and as a founding member of the Algonquin Round Table. Following the breakup of the circle, Parker traveled to Hollywood to pursue screenwriting. Her successes there, including two Academy Award nominations, were curtailed when her involvement in left-wing politics led to a place on the Hollywood blacklist.

Dismissive of her own talents, she deplored her reputation as a "wisecracker." Nevertheless, her literary output and reputation for sharp wit have endured.

In 1926, with no visible means of support, Parker went to Paris. She wrote a story to explain how this was done by saying in her typical flippant manner, "I ran off to the Riviera with a Trotskyite." It appears this Trotskyite was in reality a wealthy publisher by the name of Seward Collins. Whether it was through Collins or some other source, Parker was introduced to Otto Katz, a KGB agent. Ten years later she worked with Katz again. This time it was in the United States where they established COMM intern fronts in Hollywood and other parts of the United States.

Parker, when she returned to the United States, was arrested on different occasions as she engaged in pro-communist demonstrations. She also wrote for the Communist Party magazine, "New Masses." In 1947, the California State Senate created a fact-finding committee on Un-American activities in the State of California. As a part of their findings, they identified Dorothy Parker as a signatory or an officer of several different groups that were in fact fronts for procommunist activities.

These are only three examples of people who were "handled" by the KGB that influenced academia, the media, and entertainment in the United States. There were many others and many even today. Lenin was not only correct about the influence these three areas would have on the American public in total, but he was also correct on his approach on how to use the COMM intern and KGB agents to gain control and influence over those they could manipulate and control.

In the United States today, academia, the media, and Hollywood still spin the collectivist ideology. These three areas hold great sway over the American public. They continue to this very day to discredit capitalism and individualism as greedy and corrupt that only benefits the rich, while they sing the praises of socialism, communism, and collectivism as the way to bring social justice and total equality to the world. The United States flourished and became a beacon of light to the whole world when it was adhering to the principles established at its founding by those brave colonists who discarded collectivism for individualism.

Chapter 4. AMERICAN INDIVIDUALISM BEGINS

Individualism came about because collectivism was doing what it always does; failing. If a change had not been made, the first permanent English colony in the new world, Jamestown, would have only been a footnote in history. In April of 1607, three ships sailed 50 miles up the James River, so they would be out of view of Spanish ships. There were 144 men aboard. Many of these men were searching for fortune, but not willing to work, consequently many starved. Captain John Smith noted that the living were scarcely able to bury the dead. This forced Smith to declare the quote from the Bible, "he who will not work will not eat."

The Virginia Company, in an effort to save their colony, sent more settlers and supplies. Subsequent governors, after Smith attempted to operate the colony on a socialist model, or a model whereby all productive assets were owned by the Virginia Company and redistributed based on the perceived needs of the colonists, continued the same model. The colony continued to struggle. By 1616 more than seventeen hundred settlers had been shipped to Jamestown and The Virginia Company had spent over 50,000 pounds. All they had to show for this investment was an unprofitable town of 350 diseased and hungry colonists.

In order for the colonists to survive, and with the hope of recovering the investment and receive a positive return, two great adjustments were made. First, the Virginia

Company gave up trying to directly control the land and the employee colonists, and instead permitted the colonists to own and work land as their private property. A system was adopted that awarded 50 acres to men who were able to pay their own passage to the new world. Servants, or those who could not pay for passage, were awarded their own land after they had fulfilled their term of indenture. American capitalism was born.

John Rolfe taught the settlers how to raise tobacco. The crop thrived in Virginia, but could not be grown in England. This gave the colonists, who owned their own land and could keep the profits from the sale of tobacco, a financial incentive to expand their farms and build profitable enterprises. The lure of substantial profits for hard work and entrepreneurial ingenuity, as opposed to the initial dream of gaining a fortune by discovering some motherlode or living under a system whereby you did not have to work and could still receive, brought many people to Virginia and eventually to the other colonies.

American capitalism, a critical part of an individualistic society, was born out of necessity for survival in Jamestown. That spirit of self-reliance grew and spread throughout Virginia and then to the other colonies.

The spirit of independence and political liberty was born by accident in Massachusetts. When the Pilgrims sailed to the New World and landed in Plymouth in 1620, a bizarre twist of fate created a spirit of self-government. These Pilgrims of the Mayflower were bound for a different destination, one

500 miles south of Plymouth, but they got lost and instead landed at Plymouth in present-day Massachusetts. Since Plymouth did not lie within the boundaries of the Virginia colony, the Pilgrims had no official charter to govern them. So, they drafted the Mayflower Compact, which declared that they would rule themselves. Although Massachusetts eventually became a royal colony, the Pilgrims at Plymouth set a powerful precedent of making their own rules that later reflected itself in the town meetings that were held across colonial New England.

Within a span of less than 20 years, the American spirit that would change the world was born. In America, an individual could now become a financial success based on his ability, his efforts, and his desire. In America, an individual's financial success was not determined by his societal position at birth or because a King or Feudal Lord favored him. Regardless of his societal position at birth, an individual was able to achieve success, financial or otherwise, based on his efforts and abilities. This was unique in the world at that time.

In this same time frame, the idea of self-rule was also born. The pilgrims in Massachusetts determined that they, the people, would be sovereign and anybody who served in government would be the servant. Massachusetts, prior to the Revolution, was credited with being the hotbed of freedom. Sam Adams, often called the father of the revolution, was born and raised in Massachusetts. It was in Massachusetts that the spirit of self-rule was born, and it was in Massachusetts that it was nurtured. The desire for liberty and independence is a product of self-rule. Liberty and independence are essential for a society built on individualism or a free and independent society. Individualism was born out of necessity and not by accident. Yes, the American spirit of self-reliance and independence that changed the world, is the result. It is because of this spirit that a group of colonists declared themselves to be free and independent from what was the most powerful nation in the world at that time.

Because of this individualism and the spirit of self-reliance and independence that it generated, other people came to the New World. More colonies were established, always with freedom at the forefront; be it religious freedom, financial freedom, or freedom from other social constraints. Georgia was the 13th colony and last. It was established in 1732. James Edward Oglethorpe, a philanthropist and an English general, along with twenty-one other men, created a charter to settle this new colony and called it Georgia, after King George II. Oglethorpe spent much of his time in England working with the poor and insisted that the formation of a new colony would allow debt-ridden people a fresh start. His idea was to create an asylum for the poor and the persecuted Protestants.

Despite the growth of the colonies and the important contributions they were making to the British Empire, the long-term tensions between England, France, and Spain that led to many European conflicts, spread to the North

American continent. The Seven Years' War (called the French and Indian War in the colonies) lasted from 1756 to 1763, and had a great influence on what would become a new nation. The French no longer had a position in nearly the entirety of Eastern North America. Spain had entered the war late and was given the territory called Louisiana. A young colonist named George Washington had an inauspicious start to his military career as the head of the militia.

King George III became the King of Great Britain in 1760 and presided over the glorious conclusion of the Seven Years War. George III neither admired nor approved of the individualism in the colonies that led to their independent spirit. The colonists had grown more and more independent over time. Whether in economics, material culture, dress, language, educational institutions, professions, religions, law, or governmental institutions, the spirit that was born in Jamestown and Plymouth had become more radicalized and Americanized in the colonies.

William Pitt's policies that had won the Seven Years War and gained most of Eastern North America for the crown while pushing France from their territory east of the Mississippi, came at a huge financial cost. Those Britons at home opposed higher taxes to pay for the war. The British politicians could plainly see that the colonists had gained greatly, and determined that the Americans should share in the costs incurred for their benefit and the glory of Britain. American individualism dictated that if the Americans were to bear new taxes and responsibilities, they had to have a say in their creation. An independent people who believed in individualism, liberty and freedom, declared to King George III, "No taxation without representation." A totalitarian spirit, the spirit possessed by King George III and all totalitarians, could not tolerate a challenge to their authority.

King George, determined that it would be necessary to maintain a 10,000-man army in North America to preserve what had been won. The King and Parliament knew the British citizens could not absorb the cost of that army. In order to pay for that army, Parliament levied the Stamp Act without any colonist representation in 1765. Sam Adams said, "The Stamp-Act itself was contrived with a design only to inure the people to the habit of contemplating themselves as slaves of men; and the transition from thence to a subjection to Satan, is mighty easy."

The colonists reacted to this tax by harassing agents, destroying stamps, and refusing to enforce the law by not cooperating in any manner. Confronted with this unified and outraged opposition, Parliament backed down and repealed the Stamp-Act in 1766.

In 1773 Parliament, trying to help the East India Company who had managed to run itself into near bankruptcy, gave the East India Company a monopoly on tea sales in the colonies. At the same time, Parliament placed a small tax on the tea. Because the colonists understood they were now being compelled to purchase a product from a single supplier determined by the government, the colonists declared they would not only boycott the tea, but would prevent the tea from being unloaded in America. A group led by Sam Adams, boarded the ships that had landed in Boston Harbor with the East Indian tea and threw 342 chests of tea into the Harbor. In Delaware, nine days later, 700 chests of tea were thrown overboard and sank to the bottom of the sea.

King George III, who was naturally outraged, singled Boston as the chief culprit, and in 1774 the Intolerable or Coercive Acts were passed and specifically targeted Massachusetts. The Act closed Boston Harbor until someone paid for the tea that was destroyed, the charter of Massachusetts was annulled, the governor's council was to be appointed by the King, a new Quartering Act was passed that required homeowners and innkeepers to house soldiers at a fraction of the actual cost of boarding them, and from then on British soldiers and officials accused of committing crimes were to be returned to England for trial.

If the intent of the King and Parliament was to isolate Massachusetts from the other colonies, the Coercive Act did just the opposite. The colonists quickly learned that whatever differences they had were not as great as their similarities; individualism, self-reliance, independence, and liberty. In September of 1774, a Continental Congress was convened in Philadelphia with delegates from every colony except Georgia in attendance. The Congress passed the Galloway Plan of union. This plan proposed the establishment of a federal union for the colonies in America. Because the Galloway Plan did not declare independence from Great Britain, the colonists would not be independent from the King or Parliament. The King would have the authority to appoint the president general who would then be advised by a grand council chosen by the colonists.

The individualist spirit for independence and liberty continued to be fueled by the likes of Sam Adams from Massachusetts and Patrick Henry from Virginia. Patrick Henry called for independence on March 23, 1775, in St. John's church in Richmond, Virginia, when he proclaimed that stirring call for liberty, "It is in vain, sir, to extenuate the matter. Gentlemen may cry, Peace, Peace, but there is no peace. The war is actually begun! The next gale that sweeps from the north will bring to our ears the clash of resounding arms! Our brethren are already in the field! Why stand we here idle? What is it that gentlemen wish? What would they have? Is life so dear, or peace so sweet, as to be purchased at the price of chains and slavery? Forbid it, Almighty God! I know not what course others may take; but as for me, give me liberty or give me death!"

Sam Adams, in a speech at the Philadelphia State House on August 1, 1776 continued the same theme when he said, "If ye love wealth better than liberty, the tranquility of servitude better than the animating contest of freedom, go home from us in peace. We ask not your counsels or arms. Crouch down and lick the hands which feed you. May your chains set lightly upon you, and may posterity forget that ye were our countrymen."

"WHEN in the Course of human Events it becomes necessary for one People to dissolve the Political Bands which have connected them with another, and to assume among the Powers of the Earth the separate & equal Station to which the Laws of Nature and of Nature's God entitle them, a decent Respect to the Opinions of Mankind requires that they should declare the causes which impel them to the Separation.

WE hold these Truths to be self-evident: that all Men are created equal; that they are endowed by their creator with inherent and certain inalienable rights; that among these are life, liberty, & the pursuit of happiness: that to secure these rights, governments are instituted among men, deriving their just powers from the consent of the governed....."

The Declaration of Independence was adopted on July 4, 1776 in Philadelphia. Two weeks later Congress voted to have the statement engrossed on parchment and signed by the members. Each one of the fifty-six signers knew that the act of signing this Declaration of Independence, which in reality was also a Declaration of War, made them traitors to the Crown and subject to execution. When this Declaration of War was declared by the colonists, it was knowingly declared against perhaps the most powerful nation in the world at that time. The odds of the colonies winning their independence from Great Britain were not good. Yet the spirit of individualism, that had been developed in the colonists from as early as Jamestown and Plymouth, burned from the very depths of their being. That spirit encompassed all that Patrick Henry exclaimed in his "Give me liberty or give me death," proclamation.

Great Britain had a powerful army with much of that army already in the colonies. Great Britain had the most powerful navy in the world. Great Britain had the financial ability to support both their army and their navy. The colonists had a rag tag army at best. The colonists did not have a navy. The colonists did not have the financial resources to build either. All the colonists had was that burning spirit of individualism that demanded freedom and liberty for an independent and self-reliant people. The Revolutionary War had begun.

The miraculous happened, on October 19, 1781. British General Cornwallis surrendered 7,087 officers and men, 900 seamen, 144 cannons, 15 galleys, a frigate and 30 transport ships at a place called Yorktown, to American General George Washington. Pleading illness, Cornwallis did not attend the surrender ceremony, but his second-in-command, General Charles O'Hara, carried Cornwallis' sword to General Washington. As the British and Hessian troops marched out to surrender, the British band played the song "The World Turned Upside Down." The British had no idea how prophetic that song was; individualism had triumphed, freedom and independence had triumphed, self-reliance had triumphed. The United States of America, was born and would show the world the greatness of individualism.

Winning the war against a powerful nation like Great Britain was a great accomplishment for this upstart nation. It took a great deal of fortitude and sacrifice. By the end of the war, almost every individual who signed the Declaration of Independence or the Declaration of War, had lost property, many had lost their wives and families, and several died penniless. Yes, the ultimate price had been paid by some of the signers and so many others fighting for rights that were the province of the Creator and not man nor government. This was not lost on those who survived the war. Those who survived would now form the government for this new experiment. The reason they had paid such a price was fresh in their minds when constructing the framework that would be the government.

It was critical to these framers, that the freedom and independence they had won be preserved so individualism would prevail. When these Freedom Loving Americans sat down to create the government, they were fully aware that this new government they were creating was the single biggest threat to the freedom they had just won. Understanding the evil of government, which is the purveyor of collectivism, the framers determined to take every precaution they good to prevent this government from taking from them their freedom and independence. They also wanted to preserve this freedom for all future

Americans, but understood that the preservation of that freedom depended on those future Americans as well.

In the early years of the colonies, the King and Parliament did not pay much attention to them. The colonists were left to function largely on their own. This taught the colonists about self-rule and rule of law. It was Aristotle who said, "The only stable state is the one in which all men are equal before the law." The founders understood that rule of law must be the bedrock of their new nation.

It was Thomas Jefferson who explained the difference between rule of law and arbitrary law when he said, "Rightful liberty is unobstructed action according to our will within limits drawn around us by the equal rights of others. I do not add 'within the limits of the law' because law is often but the tyrant's will, and always so when it violates the rights of the individual."

The colonists understood the difference between rule of law and arbitrary law, between being a subject and being a citizen when King George III and Parliament determined they had the right to dictate certain taxes the colonists were to pay even though the colonists where not represented when the decision was made. The colonists again learned the differences when the King told them they must quarter his soldiers and when he told Massachusetts that those whom the King designated would not be allowed to be tried for any crime in the colonies but would be tried in England.

The Founding Fathers, learned that the rule of law is a fundamental First Principle of a free and just government. John Adams explained the Founders' understanding when he wrote that good government and the very definition of a republic "is an empire of laws."

In America, the founders declared that the government would govern the citizenry according to the law, not by the whims or fancies of any leaders. By requiring leaders to enact and publish the law, and to adhere to the same law that applies to each citizen, the rule of law was to act as a potent barrier against a tyrannical and arbitrary government.

The rule of law also requires that the same law govern all citizens. Founding Father Samuel Adams observed that the rule of law means that, "There shall be one rule of Justice for the rich and the poor; for the favorite in Court, and the Countryman at the plough."

The founders also intended that our government be limited. "The general government is not to be charged with the whole power of making and administering laws: its jurisdiction is limited to certain enumerated objects, which concern all the members of the republic, but which are not to be attained by the separate provisions of any." – James Madison, Federalist 14, 1787

In Article 1, Section 8. Of the United States Constitution, we find the enumerated objects to which the government is limited:

The Congress shall have Power To lay and collect Taxes, Duties, Imposts and Excises, to pay the Debts and provide for the common Defense and general Welfare of the United States; but all Duties, Imposts and Excises shall be uniform throughout the United States. There are 26 enumerated powers. We will discuss them later.

The founders wanted to be sure there was no misunderstanding that the Federal government was to be limited. As a part of the Bill of Rights they included the 10th Amendment which reinforces the limitations of the federal government. The 10th Amendment states, "The powers not delegated to the United States by the Constitution, nor prohibited by it to the States, are reserved to the States respectively, or to the people."

There can be no doubt that the founders intended to limit the Federal government. The founders understood that an unlimited government would come to control the lives and the thoughts of the citizens. The founders understood that big government always leads to tyrannical government. The founders understood that big government always leads to collectivism.

James Madison explained the evils of large government when he stated, "If Congress can do whatever in their discretion can be done by money, and will promote the General Welfare, the Government is no longer a limited one, possessing enumerated powers, but an indefinite one, subject to particular exceptions."

As critical as it was to have a government of laws adhering to the concept of rule of law and to have a limited government that exercises only those powers specifically granted to it, the founders also understood that power must be divested and not concentrated. They created a government with three separate branches of government that had checks and balances, one against the other.

"An elective despotism was not the government we fought for; but one in which the powers of government should be so divided and balanced among the several bodies of magistracy as that no one could transcend their legal limits without being effectually checked and restrained by the others." – James Madison, Federalist 84, 1788

"The accumulation of all powers, legislative, executive, and judiciary, in the same hands, whether of one, a few, or many, and whether hereditary, self-appointed, or elective, may justly be pronounced the very definition of tyranny." – James Madison, Federalist 47, 1788

"The principle of the Constitution is that of a separation of Legislative, Executive and Judiciary functions, except in cases specified. If this principle be not expressed in direct terms, it is clearly the spirit of the Constitution... "– Thomas Jefferson, letter to James Madison, 1797

The founders declared that the United States of America would be a nation with the people as the sovereign and those in government would be the servant. This was the opposite of what the world knew at that time. People were to be servants to the King, Emperor, or Czar. Our founders said it is governments purpose to serve the people.

Thomas Jefferson explained why this was so important to protecting freedom when he said, "When governments fear the people, there is liberty. When the people fear the government, there is tyranny. The strongest reason for the people to retain the right to keep and bear arms is, as a last resort, to protect themselves against tyranny in government."

In the Declaration of Independence, the founders noted "That to secure these rights, Governments are instituted among Men, deriving their just powers from the consent of the governed." The Preamble to the United States Constitution begins, "We the People of the United States, in order to form a more perfect Union……"

The United State of America was founded as an individualist nation where individual rights are paramount, property is that of the individual and not the state, and each individual has the right to pursue his own happiness, strive to reach his full potential, achieve his dreams, be self-reliant, and live as a free and independent individual. The individual would not have to, nor would they be expected to limit their dreams and desires because the collective would disagree with those dreams or desires, it was deemed by the collective not to be in its best interest, or the individual's achievements were deemed to be detrimental to the ego or self-image of others.

The founders protected this freedom by instituting a government with four critical principals; rule of law, limited government, divided government, and sovereignty of the people with the government as the servant. To the degree these principles would be altered would be the degree to which the rights of individuals would be limited and even disappear; arbitrary law would replace rule of law with certain individuals being treated differently under the law; limited government would be replaced with big tyrannical government; divided government would be changed where power would become concentrated, and the roles of government and the people would be reversed where government would become sovereign and the people would become servants.

Chapter 5. RULE OF LAW

In the early years of the colonies, the King and Parliament did not pay much attention to them. The colonists were left to function largely on their own. This taught them about self-rule and rule of law. It was Aristotle who said, "The only stable state is the one in which all men are equal before the law."

It was Thomas Jefferson who explained the difference between rule of law and arbitrary law when he said, "Rightful liberty is unobstructed action according to our will within limits drawn around us by the equal rights of others. I do not add 'within the limits of the law' because law is often but the tyrant's will, and always so when it violates the rights of the individual."

The colonists understood the difference between rule of law and arbitrary law, between being a subject and being a citizen when King George III and Parliament determined they had the right to dictate certain taxes the colonists were to pay even though the colonists where not represented when the decision was made. The colonists again learned the differences when the King told them they must quarter his soldiers and when he told Massachusetts that those whom the King designated would not be allowed to be tried for any crime in the colonies but would be tried in England.

The Founding Fathers, learned that the rule of law is a fundamental First Principle of a free and just government. John Adams explained the Founders' understanding when he wrote that good government and the very definition of a republic "is an empire of laws."

In America, the founders declared that the government would govern according to the law, not by the whims or fancies of any leaders. Prior to this declaration, most governments governed according to the wishes of the King, the Emperor, or the Czar. His or her statement was final, until he or she decided the old law was to be abandoned or changed and his or her new statement was now the law. By requiring leaders to enact and publish the law, and to adhere to the same law that applies to each citizen, the rule of law was to act as a barrier against tyrannical and arbitrary government.

The rule of law also requires that the same law govern all citizens, even those who made the law, including Kings, Emperors, or Czars. As we have noted before, Samuel Adams stated this principle when he said that the rule of law means that, "There shall be one rule of Justice for the rich and the poor; for the favorite in court, and the Countryman at the plough."

It was eleven years after the Declaration of Independence—and six years after American victory in the Revolutionary War—that a small group of delegates would come together, again in Philadelphia, to write a constitution that would govern their new nation. To understand this incredible achievement, we must understand that nothing like this had ever been done before. The document that was produced, The Constitution of the United States of America, was created based on the great foundational principle of rule of law.

Rule of law has been called the most significant and influential accomplishment of Western constitutional thinking. The very meaning and structure of our Constitution embody this principle. You will not read the phrase "rule of law" in the Constitution, yet it is evident throughout the Constitution. Rule of law is the rock upon which the American legal and political system was built, indeed it is the very essence of American society.

Throughout most of history, the law or rules by which societies were governed were determined by the sword and deceit: he who had the power—whether military strength or political dominance—made the rules. The command of the King, the Emperor, the Czar, or the absolute monarch or tyrannical despot was the rule, it was the law. These despots or tyrants concocted false stories of inheritance and rationalizations, most often "divine right," to convince the people that they, the people, were to accept the rule of the tyrant or despot without question. Even today this is still the case in many parts of the world, such as North Korea, where the arbitrary rulings of the dictator are the law.

A principle that came long before the Constitution of the United States, was that the rule of law is the general concept that the governors as well as the governed, are subject to the same law and that all are to be equally protected by the law. This principle can be found as early as the writings of Plato and Aristotle. We learn that the practice of the principle of equal protection under the law was not common place prior to the Constitution, and is not always practiced even today.

In English history, this principle was expressed in Magna Carta in 1215. In the thirty-ninth clause, King John promised that "No free man shall be taken, imprisoned, disseized, outlawed, or banished, or in any way destroyed, nor will he proceed against or prosecute him, except by the lawful judgment of his peers and the Law of the Land." The principle that the law is above human rulers has been the cornerstone of English constitutional law since.

The American colonists had been reminded of this principle through different writers. Thomas Paine restated this idea dramatically in Common Sense:

"But where says some is the king of America? I'll tell you Friend, he reigns above, and doth not make havoc of mankind like the Royal of Britain. Yet that we may not appear to be defective even in earthly honors, let a day be solemnly set apart for proclaiming the charter; let it be brought forth placed on the divine law, the word of God; let a crown be placed thereon, by which the world may know, that so far as we approve of monarchy, that in America THE LAW IS KING. For as in absolute governments the King is law, so in free countries the law ought to be king; and there ought to be no other. But lest any ill use should afterwards arise, let the crown at the conclusion of the ceremony be demolished, and scattered among the people whose right it is."

John Adams expressed this idea so classically when he wrote the Massachusetts Constitution in 1780, in which the powers of the commonwealth are divided in the document "to the end it may be a government of laws, not of men." It is hard to come up with a simpler definition.

Over time, the rule of law had come to be associated with four key components. First, the rule of law means a formal, regular process of law enforcement and adjudication. What we really mean by "a government of laws, not of men" is the rule of men is bound by law, not subject to the arbitrary will of others. Under rule of law, the King could not exempt a family member or friend from being tried for the same crime for which another person was tried. The rule of law means general rules of law that bind all people and are known and enforced by a system of courts and law enforcement, not by mere arbitrary authority.

So that equal rights are given to all citizens, it is the duty of government to apply law fairly and equally through a legal and consistent process such as notice, hearings, indictment, trial by jury, legal counsel, and the right against self-incrimination. In the United States this process is protected by the Constitution. American citizens are to have these regular procedural protections and have safeguards against abuse by government authority. One of the complaints lodged against George III in the Declaration of Independence, was that he had "obstructed the administration of justice, by refusing his assent to laws for establishing judiciary powers," and was "depriving us in many cases, of the benefits of trial by jury."

Second, the rule of law means that these rules are binding on rulers, including government, and the ruled, or we the people, alike. If the American people, Madison wrote in Federalist 57, "shall ever be so far debased as to tolerate a law not obligatory on the legislature, as well as on the people, the people will be prepared to tolerate anything but liberty." As all are subject to the law, so all—government and citizens, indeed all persons—are equal before the law, and equally subject to the legal system and its decisions. No one is above the law in respect to enforcement; no one is privileged to ignore the law, just as no one is outside the law in terms of its protection. As is often said, all are presumed innocent until proven guilty. This equal application of laws is reflected in the Constitution's references to "citizens" and "persons" rather than race, class, or some other group distinction. In the 5th Amendment it says, "No person shall . . . be deprived of life, liberty, or property, without due process of law." It is again in the 14th Amendment's guarantee that "No State shall . . . deny to any person within its jurisdiction the equal protection of the laws." The rights of all are dependent on the rights of each being defended and protected. The rule of law is an expression of—no, it is a requirement of—the idea of each person possessing equal rights by nature. That again is each person or individual, not a class or group.

Next, the rule of law implies that there are certain unwritten rules or generally understood standards to which specific laws and lawmaking must conform. There are some things that no government legitimately, based on the rule of law, can do. Many of these implications came about over the course of British history. Many of these same implications can be seen in the clauses of the U.S. Constitution. There can be no "ex post facto" laws—that is, laws that classify an act as a crime leading to punishment after the act occurs. Nor can there be "bills of attainder," which are laws that punish people without a judicial trial. There is writ of "habeas corpus" or no person may be imprisoned without legal cause, and the rule against "double jeopardy" or no person can be tried or punished twice for the same crime.

Lastly, courts and judges are the administrators of rule of law, but the rule of law is ultimately based on lawmaking and who has that authority. Although we have three branches of government with checks and balances, the legislature is the only branch given the authority to make law. Those who make law are themselves subject to higher authority. The Declaration of Independence states that certain rights come from the Creator. These rights do not come from man nor government. This means there are different types of laws, some of which are more significant and important and consequently have more authority. The concept of rule of law is one of these. It is a definite restraint on government. It judges government based on a higher standard. They do not change day to day or by the whim of the moment and cannot be altered by acts of government.

The definition of arbitrary law could be defined as that law determined or founded on individual discretion, especially when based on one's opinion, judgment, or prejudice, rather than on fixed rules, procedures, or law. (1)

The rule of law is the legal principle that states that nobody, not even a king, president or prime minister, is above the law. Before rule of law, arbitrary law existed where Kings, Emperors, Czars, and other people in power would act without impunity. Because the rule of law is such a core concept of the American system of government, many believe it is always practiced in the United States and faces no threat from arbitrary law. In addition, arbitrary law is generally likened to some form of monarchy.

Arbitrary law is commonly associated with what was and is known as the divine right of kings. The idea of the divine right of kings was widely accepted throughout Europe and other parts of the world. This principle sees society as highly hierarchical, with the monarch at the top of the pyramid, the sovereign, and closest to God. It was commonly held that God had placed the monarch in his position of power and as a result, the monarch's authority was sanctioned by God. In some situations, there were some limits on the monarch's authority, but the divine right of kings meant that the monarch's word was law, even in life and death situations. Ivan the Terrible and Peter the Great both killed their sons. Henry the VIII had Anne Boleyn, his second wife beheaded. These acts went unpunished because the monarch was considered to be above the law.

Another form of arbitrary law would be rule of man. This is when people do not claim divine rule, but govern a society or a country after they have acquired power through a revolution or coup. In recent times, the rule of man is best exemplified by the totalitarian states, such as Adolf Hitler's Germany or Joseph Stalin's USSR. In such states, power was arbitrarily wielded by either a dictator or a small group of individuals who were treated as being above the law. There dictates were treated as law and if questioned, serious ramifications were the result, including torture and/or death.

Sometimes the rule of man does not have to take the form of monarchs or dictators; rather, the majority of the population can form its own sort of totalitarian rule. Ochlocracy, also known as mob rule, is when the law becomes subverted to the demands of the populace. Ochlocracy is often a state where emotions trump reason and logic. While the United States has never been controlled by an ochlocracy per se, there have been some notable instances where the rule of law was subjugated to the rule of the mob. For example, during the Salem witch trials, in the American west mobs would lynch individuals without trials, and in the American South mobs were often set against runaway slaves, and later, ethnic minorities in the form of lynching's that were outside the purview of the law.

Although in the United States we no longer see our rule of law being subverted by mob lynching's, we do see mob rule used. Most recently mob rule has been used under the euphemism of "protest." Certain groups, to make a point, sometimes specific and sometimes vague, will take to the streets and enforce their own laws by rioting, destroying public and private property, stealing and looting, and causing bodily harm even to the point of death. The same actions occur when certain groups, in the name of free speech, take it upon themselves to riot, destroy public and private property, steal and loot, and cause bodily harm even to the point of death. In both these situations the rule of law is subverted, and arbitrary law occurs with the mob dictating the law.

Rule of law depends also on the law being applied equally to all persons regardless of the persons position in government, position in society, economic status, ethnicity, color of skin, or religion. The rule of law is subverted for instance when congress exempts itself or any other group from the ramifications of any law it passes. When any branch of law enforcement, be it federal, state, or local refuses to apply the same standards for indictment from one person to another, the rule of law is being subverted. For instance, if a lowly member of the armed services, or a staff worker for a government agency, is indicted and tried for treason because they have violated the law applying to the handling of classified government information, but a cabinet member is held to another standard even though they violated the same law, this is subverting the rule of law.

In any of these situations where we do not adhere to the rule of law for whatever reason, we are moving from that critical standard to the lesser and easily manipulated standard of arbitrary law. Our founders had lived under a form of arbitrary law prior to winning their freedom. They made rule of law a bedrock principle in our nation. They did this because they wanted to live as free people for the entirety of their existence and it was their goal that the United States exist as a free nation forever. In order for that to happen the founders understood that future Americans would have to protect the concept of rule of law.

A nation of free and independent people can only exist if the principle of rule of law is strictly observed in that nation. Up until the United States gained its freedom, no nation had truly adhered to the principle of rule of law. Up until the United States gained its freedom, the citizens of any country had never truly been free and independent. Up until the United States gained its freedom, no nation had come under the doctrine of individualism. Individualism, again, is when the rights of the individual are protected. The rights of the individual are protected when the law is published and known, when due process is followed, and when the law is applied equally to all individuals regardless of position or other classification.

As a society or nation allows rule of law to morph into arbitrary law, it also allows freedom and independence to morph into totalitarianism and dictatorship, it allows individualism to morph into collectivism. Remember, collectivism is when the rights of the individual are subjugated to what is determined to be for the good of the collective or the good of society. What is determined to be for the good of the collective or the good of society is itself arbitrary. The collectivist defines good based on arbitrary standards.

Collectivism can only exist under arbitrary law. Because "for the good of the collective" is determined on a sliding scale, the collectivist needs the flexibility to enforce a law based on the needs at any point in time. Society cannot exist with constant rioting, destroying public and private property, stealing and looting, and causing bodily harm even to the point of death. The collectivist determines that these actions are necessary and must be tolerated at certain times to make certain statements. Even though laws exist that deem these actions to be unlawful, the collectivist ignores those laws to make their statement they have determined is for the good of the collective. The rights of the individual are ignored; thus, collectivism is substituted for individualism as arbitrary law is substituted for rule of law.

The collectivist may determine that the good of the collective is paramount when a person is shot by a police officer, regardless of the extenuating circumstances, so they revert to arbitrary law. The collectivist may determine that what an individual is going to freely say is not in the best interest of the collective, so the collectivist reverts to arbitrary law. A collectivist may determine that the laws that were passed are not applicable to members of certain groups such as government, so they revert to arbitrary law. A collectivist may determine that an individual, because of position, political philosophy, family affiliation, or any other reason is not to be treated equally under the law, so they revert to arbitrary law.

In these situations, the reverting to arbitrary law is denouncing the basics of freedom and independence. Freedom and independence are a product of rule of law and individualism is a product of rule of law. They are interdependent, and our founders knew this. That is why they made rule of law a cornerstone of our nation.

The collectivist also understands this rule. The collectivist believes the collective supersedes the individual and what is good for the collective is always best for society. The collectivist does not believe in individual rights, and any rights extended to the individual is at the behest of the collective or government. The collectivist understands that good is evasive, so flexibility is necessary. The collectivist understands that rule of law does not allow for this necessary flexibility. Arbitrary law has always served the needs of the collectivist as has totalitarianism. Under both, the collectivist can react quickly, so they can implement the necessary laws to bring about the new idea of what they have determined is for the good of the collective. Collectivism can only work under arbitrary law. Collectivism can only work under some form of totalitarianism. Collectivism, arbitrary law, and totalitarianism are dependent one on the other.

It is primarily the judiciary branch of our government that is responsible to see to it that we as a nation adhere to rule of law. Without a doubt, all citizens have a responsibility to live by the precepts of rule of law as well as hold our judiciary and other government servants to these same principles.

The Constitution says, "The judicial Power of the United States, shall be vested in one supreme Court, and in such inferior Courts as the Congress may from time to time ordain and establish." In the Federalist Papers, Alexander Hamilton referred to the judiciary as the least dangerous branch of government, stating that judges under the Constitution would possess "neither force nor will, but merely judgment."

Today it is commonly believed that the role of the Judiciary Branch is to interpret the Constitution and limit the powers of the other branches of government. The Supreme Court's usurped power to do this is its assumed power of judicial review, where it determines which laws and policies are constitutional, or allowable, and which are not. This was not the stated role of the Judiciary Branch in Article III of the Constitution, nor was it the intended role per the Federalist Papers. This improperly assumed role of the judiciary has diminished the concepts of rule of law and it has encouraged judges to rule as if they were under the divine role concept. Consequently, the Judiciary branch has usurped to often the legislative role of the Legislative Branch as well as the executive role of the Executive Branch. But more about this when we discuss the importance of diffused power in another chapter.

The founders created our government so that the freedom they had just won would be protected for them and for all future generations of Americans. In order to assure this protection, they adopted the concept of rule of law. The term rule of law refers to a principle of governance in which all persons, institutions and entities, public and private, including the state itself, are accountable to laws that are publicly promulgated, equally enforced, and independently adjudicated.

This concept was new to the world and not common at that time. Most, if not all, governments at that time adhered to what is commonly called arbitrary law. Under arbitrary law, the law applies to certain entities, it is not necessarily publicly known or even written, and it is not evenly or independently adjudicated. It was more common in most countries to have rulers who were considered to have divine right, and so they were the law.

A critical concept under rule of law is that the burden of proof lies with the state as opposed to the defendant. Under arbitrary law, if the state accuses a citizen of committing a crime, the state does not have to prove guilt. The citizen has the duty of proving innocence. Our founders declared that the burden of proof in our system would lie with the state. The defense is not even required to present a case if they believe the state has not adequately proven guilt. This is referred to as burden of proof and determines where that obligation of proof lies. The founders clearly understood that burden of proof being the obligation of the state was an important protector of freedom and the rights of the individual or individualism.

Over time, the proponents of collectivism have confused the American public regarding this critical concept. In America today, it is a commonly held belief that the constitution says that people are innocent until proven guilty. This is a preposterous statement without rational meaning. Actual guilt or innocence has nothing to do with a court or even rule of law or arbitrary law. An individual has either committed the act and is therefore guilty or they have not and is therefore innocent. Any ruling or verdict rendered by any court does not change the fact of guilt or innocence. The defense attorneys and collectivist citizens want the public to belief the phrase, innocent until proven guilty is literal. The importance of this concept is the presumption of guilt or innocence and consequently upon whom burden of proof is placed, the state or the citizen. In a free and independent society adhering to individualism, the defendant is presumed to be innocent by the court, and the burden of proof must lie with the state. In a totalitarian state that adheres to collectivism, the defendant is presumed to be guilty and the burden of proof lies with the defendant. An example of the assumption of guilt and the burden of proof lying with the defendant in the United

States today would be the policy whereby police can seize money and property from suspected criminals, even if they have not been or are never charged or convicted. This is not rule of law. The acceptance of this type of policy is moving our nation from individualism to collectivism.

A very critical element of rule of law is that the law is to be written and made known to the public so that rulings are rendered based on what the law states. Kings, Emperors, and Czars, proclaimed themselves to be appointed by God and thus they had divine rights. Having divine rights and being appointed by God, they assumed the role of knowing intent, even if their presumed knowledge was different from what was written. Our Judiciary Branch, specifically members of the Supreme Court, Appellate Courts, and even District Courts have claimed divine rights when determining their rulings based on what they deemed to be intent and not what was written.

The Chief Justice of the Supreme Court recently determined that the word "penalty" really meant "tax." The law clearly read "penalty." The regime responsible stated publicly that it was meant to be penalty when speaking to the public. Only when the regime argued before the Supreme Court did they say that "penalty" was intended to read "tax." The Chief Justice assumed the position of divine right and determined that "penalty" really means "tax." The Chief Justice of the Supreme Court, acting under the doctrine of divine right as opposed to following the concept of rule of law, violated the core of the concept of rule of law and applied arbitrary law.

This same Chief Justice of the Supreme Court than determined that those writing laws, including members of congress, do not understand that a capital S in front of the word State gives it an entirely different meaning from when the word state begins with a small s. The law that gave us Obamacare clearly had "State" written and not "state." The Chief Justice again assumed divinity as would a King, an Emperor, or a Czar and said he in fact knew that state was intended even though State was written. He again violated a core principle of rule of law. The Chief Justice of the Supreme Court of the United States of America moved the United States from being a free and independent nation, an adherent to individualism, closer to totalitarianism and collectivism adhering to arbitrary law.

This idea of a judge assuming divine right has transcended to all courts. Today we have district and appellate judges determining that a legally written declaration by the executive does not meet their standards, and because they have determined they are divine, they knew the clear intent of the author. Remember, the divine judge had heard words from this author on the campaign trail, and they, having divine insight, understood the authors heart and his intent. This is a clear violation of the concept rule of law.

Defense attorneys and juries also violate core principles of rule of law. Under rule of law, all members of the court system, including defense attorneys are to have as their core principle to be a seeker of the truth. The defense attorney is to provide the best defense he can for his client, even if that means he determines it is the best defense of his client not to present a defense. What the defense attorney is not supposed to do is to clearly lie or mislead in his vigorous pursuit of the truth. Yet, it has become common practice to see defense attorneys lie, manipulate, twist, and mislead. One of the more infamous examples was when an infamous defense attorney clearly presented fiction as fact when he alluded to Columbian Drug Lords killing two innocent people when all the factual evidence pointed to his celebrity defendant. As bad as this violation of rule of law was, a clearly incapable and intimidated judge allowed the farce to continue. Under rule of law, we are to seek the truth. Arbitrary law allows lies, misleading statements, twisting, and manipulation. The totalitarian state is allowed to do whatever is necessary to achieve their desired result.

Citizens also have a critical role to play to maintain a free and independent state that adheres to individualism. Under rule of law, all parties have the right to be tried by a jury of impartial jurors whose only purpose is to listen to the facts and render an impartial verdict. The jury is not given the freedom to determine their verdict based on who the defendant is, the race of the defendant, or any other such factor. The jury has the responsibility to treat the trial as if it were in a vacuum. The jury is not to allow any outside factors to weigh on their judgement. Those factors would include such things as the state of race relations or the outcome of any previous trial. The jury does not have the right, under rule of law, to render a verdict to advance some social agenda. Their only purpose is to render a fair and impartial verdict based on the specific facts pertaining to the specific case. Any advocate of so called "jury nullification" for any reason, is in fact destroying the concept of rule of law and advancing arbitrary law. They are nullifying individualism and proclaiming collectivism. They are denying freedom and independence and supporting totalitarianism.

Freedom and independence has been a fleeting concept. It is difficult to attain but simple to lose. The founders knew rule of law was critical to freedom and independence. Rule of law is critical to individualism. These two facts cannot be repeated enough. Nor can it be said enough, how our nation is now willingly substituting the principles of rule of law for the politically correct and socially just standards of arbitrary law. The result can only be loss of freedom and independence and loss of individualism. The only other possibility when rule of law is gone, is totalitarianism which incorporates arbitrary law and collectivism.

Rule of law is only applicable to free and independent societies. Arbitrary law is only applicable to totalitarian societies. Our founders protected their freedom and our freedom by implementing rule of law. The very branch of government, the Judiciary Branch, who is most responsible to protect the concept of rule of law, is leading the charge to eradicate rule of law and apply arbitrary law. The

Judiciary Branch is an important and major player in the promise to fundamentally transform the United States from a free and independent nation to a Collectivist totalitarian state. The judiciary branch advances that transformation every time they violate rule of law, wittingly or unwitting.

(1) Three Alternatives to the Rule of Law, written by Christi Hayes and Fact Checked by The Law Dictionary Staff

Law Dictionary: The Four Pillars of the Rule of Law Written by Christi Hayes

Chapter 6. LIMITED GOVERNMENT

After the Revolutionary War had been won, the founders began the equally difficult task of creating a government that would protect the freedom they had just won. They clearly understood that any government they would form would always be the single biggest threat to that freedom. They clearly understood that government always tends to grow and with that growth comes the desire for power and control by those whose proper role was intended to be servant and not sovereign. The founders understood human nature and the desire of one human to control and rule another.

Patrick Henry said, "The Constitution is not an instrument for the government to restrain the people, it is an instrument for the people to restrain the government - lest it (the government) come to dominate our lives and interests."

"The general government is not to be charged with the whole power of making and administering laws: its jurisdiction is limited to certain enumerated objects, which concern all the members of the republic, but which are not to be attained by the separate provisions of any." – James Madison, Federalist 14, 1787

The intent of the founders concerning the role of the United States Constitution was to limit the role of government. In the United States the people were to be the sovereign and it was the people who would grant power or rights to the government as opposed to having government grant rights to the people. We the people granted to The United States government limited powers; we granted to the government 26 enumerated powers.

In Article 1, Section 8. Of the United States Constitution, we find the enumerated objects to which the government is limited:

The Congress shall have Power To lay and collect Taxes, Duties, Imposts and Excises, to pay the Debts and provide for the common Defence and general Welfare of the United States; but all Duties, Imposts and Excises shall be uniform throughout the United States.

There can be no doubt that the founders intended to limit the Federal government. The founders understood that an unlimited government would come to control the lives, thoughts, and interests of the citizens. The founders understood that big government always leads to tyrannical government. The founders understood that big government always leads to collectivism.

James Madison explained the evils of large government when he stated, "If Congress can do whatever in their discretion can be done by money, and will promote the General Welfare, the Government is no longer a limited one, possessing enumerated powers, but an indefinite one, subject to particular exceptions."

This is the list of enumerated powers of the federal constitution which James Madison specified:

The Congress shall have Power To lay and collect Taxes, Duties, Imposts and Excises, to pay the Debts and provide for the common Defense and general Welfare of the United States; but all Duties, Imposts and Excises shall be uniform throughout the United States;

To borrow on the credit of the United States;

To regulate Commerce with foreign Nations, and among the several States, and with the Indian Tribes;

To establish a uniform Rule of Naturalization, and uniform Laws on the subject of Bankruptcies throughout the United States;

To coin Money, regulate the Value thereof, and of foreign Coin, and fix the Standard of Weights and Measures;

To provide for the Punishment of counterfeiting the Securities and current Coin of the United States;

To establish Post Offices and Post Roads;

To promote the Progress of Science and useful Arts, by securing for limited Times to Authors and Inventors the exclusive Right to their respective Writings and Discoveries;

To constitute Tribunals inferior to the supreme Court;

To define and punish Piracies and Felonies committed on the high Seas, and Offenses against the Law of Nations;

To declare War, grant Letters of Marque and Reprisal, and make Rules concerning Captures on Land and Water;

To raise and support Armies, but no Appropriation of Money to that Use shall be for a longer Term than two Years;

To provide and maintain a Navy;

To make Rules for the Government and Regulation of the land and naval Forces;

To provide for calling forth the Militia to execute the Laws of the Union, suppress Insurrections and repel Invasions;

To provide for organizing, arming, and disciplining, the Militia, and for governing such Part of them as may be employed in the Service of the United States, reserving to the States respectively, the Appointment of the Officers, and the Authority of training the Militia according to the discipline prescribed by Congress;

To exercise exclusive Legislation in all Cases whatsoever, over such District (not exceeding ten Miles square) as may, by Cession of particular States, and the acceptance of Congress, become the Seat of the Government of the United States, and to exercise like Authority over all Places purchased by the Consent of the Legislature of the State in which the Same shall be, for the Erection of Forts, Magazines, Arsenals, dock-Yards, and other needful Buildings; And

To make all Laws which shall be necessary and proper for carrying into Execution the foregoing Powers, and all other

Powers vested by this Constitution in the Government of the United States, or in any Department or Officer thereof.

The founders wanted to be sure there was no misunderstanding that the Federal government was to be limited. As a part of the Bill of Rights they included the 10th Amendment, which reinforces the limitations of the federal government. The 10th Amendment states, "The powers not delegated to the United States by the Constitution, nor prohibited by it to the States, are reserved to the States respectively, or to the people."

One of the primary reasons the colonists revolted from Great Britain was because of the evil of big government. It was big government that told the colonists they must house or quarter the governments soldiers in their homes and receive about 25% of the actual cost for this government mandated imposition. So not only did big government say we will require you to suffer this imposition, but you will also bear the cost of said imposition.

It was big government that told the colonists that big government must have more of the colonist's money and that the colonists would not have a say in the law that became known as 'The Stamp Act." Big government imposed many different taxes on the colonists including the taxes that were a part of The Stamp Act without any input from the colonists. The reaction of the colonists was to refuse to accept this demand placed upon them under the now famous statement, "no taxation without representation."

Big government than said to the colonists that they were going to use the power of government to pick a corporate winner and require that the only company from whom the colonists could purchase their tea would be the British East India Tea Company. Big government had now placed itself in the position of picking corporate winners and losers and not allowing the marketplace to perform this function.

After the colonists said no to "crony capitalism" and threw the tea aboard the ships of big governments chosen winner into the harbors, big government told the colonists they would punish the colonists of Massachusetts until somebody paid for the tea. In addition, big government told these colonists that they would have no say in those who were now in charge of governing them. The colonists were also told that the law would be administered differently. Some people, those determined by big government, would be subject to different standards, rules, and laws. These specially determined colonists would not be tried in courts in the colonies for crimes committed in the colonies, but these special people would be tried for those crimes in Great Britain under the rules and standards determined appropriate by the Great Britain Courts.

The colonists had been victims of the evils of big government and clearly understood how big government threatens freedom and liberty of the individual.

Limited government is essential for a nation based on individualism because limited government values individual and economic freedom. Less government means less intrusion into our lives. This is what Patrick Henry meant when he said it was the intent and function of the Constitution, to not allow government to dominate our lives and our thoughts. Government regulations and mandates are immanent in big government. Limited government frees us from excessive regulation or mandates, and that means that citizens can make more choices on an individual and financial level for themselves. We can live our lives as we see fit, not how bureaucrats or the government sees fit. People can act and live according to their own way of thinking and not by government mandate.

Under limited government, it is the expectation that the individual will be left alone to live their lives. The right to privacy and personal freedom comes with the understanding that our individual rights end as soon as they infringe upon another individual's rights. Freedom and liberty means that we do not have a government agency telling us what we can and should eat, what kind of cars we can and should drive, or what kind of health policy we can and should have. The individual is left with the responsibility of his or her own decisions and actions. Collectivism with big government tells you where you can live, what kind of house you can have, what course of study you must take, and what kind of health insurance you must have.

Limited government also means freedom in the market place. The less the government gets involved in the marketplace, the more businesses can thrive and create a competitive and innovative atmosphere. Competition, innovation, and the profit motive is what drives companies and offers products to consumers at all price points. Competition and profit motive, are what drives companies to improve their product, make it more cost-effective, and offer impeccable customer service. As companies prosper and make profits, these profits are re-invested in the business for purposes of growth, and jobs are created.

In a collectivist nation the bureaucrats believe they can determine better what should be produced and how it should be produced. The government starts over-regulating and businesses are given untold layers of paperwork required by government to prove the company complies. Profits that could have and should have been re-invested into creating more jobs is wasted on compliance requirements. As the cost of doing business goes up, so does the cost of the product or service.

For every regulation, mandate or requirement, more government employees need to be hired to ensure compliance. The consumer pays twice because of these government controls; once for the increased cost of the product and second for the salaries and benefits of the government employee.

Bureaucrats, who are supposed to be servants but assume the role of sovereign, continue to impose more and more regulations. These regulations are treated by the courts and the executive branch as if they were law. The executive branch has thus usurped the role of the legislative branch since the constitution only gives the legislative branch the authority to make law.

The over regulating government assumes the role of a central planner. A critical role played by government in any collectivist nation is the role of central planner. Just as collectivists believe it is the role of government to dictate to individuals how they are to live their lives and how they are to think, the collectivist also believes the government can and should dictate how companies should run their business by telling them how they are to treat their employees, what they are to produce, how much they are to produce, and the maximum profit they can make.

The founders understood that limited government creates an environment of independence and individualism. When government assumes that it is best equipped to solve a problem, the problem inevitably becomes worse instead of better. Nothing is done to alleviate the core of the problem it set out to solve. This is perhaps best exhibited when government determined it was best equipped to solve what it determined to be a poverty problem and "declared war on poverty." Numerous and duplicative programs were set up as safety nets. The benefits provided by these programs became a way of life to far too many individuals. The benefits are now considered a constitutional right by collectivists. They have had no impact on reducing poverty but have been instrumental in destroying the key structure of individualism, the family.

These unconstitutional redistribution programs, essential to collectivism, were initiated as a reaction to a perceived problem and did not consider the long-term consequences or the effect on the community. As is always the case when transferring from individualism to collectivism, the government programs start small, but grow until those who they were meant to help, become completely dependent upon the government instead of themselves. The long-term effect is government programs deny people the ability to live their lives as they see fit. The long-term effect is victims of these programs become slaves to the government, become subject to generational dependency and poverty, and believe their only option is collectivism.

These collectivist government programs do more harm than good when they take away an individual's inalienable right to life, liberty, and the pursuit of happiness, as detailed in the Declaration of Independence, because they are caught up in a collectivist system they cannot escape. This is the intent of collectivists. A collectivist understands that when people are the recipient of redistributed government aid, they live with the inevitably destructive fear of "what the government gives, the government can take away."

The individualist understands that the only way for people to live a fulfilling life – one that they create, one that they choose – is to live under an individualist government that limits its infringement on the daily lives of citizens. A limited government is the one that offers its citizens the right to individual and economic freedom with the liberty to pursue their lives as they see fit.

Limited government is a critical element of freedom, liberty, and individualism. Our founding fathers understood this was so. Consequently, our founding fathers, as a part of the constitution, declared that the government of the United States was to be a limited government. The founding fathers understood that big government destroys freedom and liberty by destroying the individual, the family, and the community. The founding fathers effectively told us that if we wanted to pass the freedom and liberty they had given us, unto future Americans, it would be essential that we limit the government to the powers in the constitution. If we did that, we would maintain a government based on individualism; a government that would not "come to dominate our lives and our interests."

Chapter 7. DIVIDED GOVERNMENT

"If the three powers maintain their mutual independence on each other our Government may last long, but not so if either can assume the authorities of the other." --Thomas Jefferson

America's Founders had just declared themselves free from a tyrannical government. They were determined that such tyranny would never be repeated in this land. Their new charter of government – the Constitution – carefully defined the powers delegated to government. The Founders were determined to bind down the administrators of the federal government with Constitutional chains so that abuse of power in any of its branches would be prevented. The revolutionary idea of separation of powers, although unpopular at first, became a means by which this was to be accomplished.

John Adams, in a letter to Dr. Benjamin Rush, stated: "I call you to witness that I was the first member of Congress who ventured to come out in public, as I did in January 1776, in my 'Thoughts on Government,' ...in favor of a government with three branches, and an independent judiciary..." By the time the Constitution was adopted, the idea was supported by all the members of the Convention. James Madison, the father of the Constitution, devoted five Federalist Papers (47-51) to an explanation of how the Executive, Legislative, and Judicial branches were to be wholly independent of each other, yet bound together through an intricate system of checks and balances. Madison believed that keeping the three branches separated was fundamental to the preservation of liberty. He wrote:

"The accumulation of all powers, legislative, executive, and judiciary, in the same hands, whether of one, a few, or many... may justly be pronounced the very definition of tyranny."

George Washington, in his Farewell Address, reminded Americans of the need to preserve the Founders' system. He spoke of the "love of power and proneness to abuse it which predominates in the human heart" and warned of the "necessity of reciprocal checks of political power, by dividing and distributing it into different depositories and constituting each the guardian ... against invasions by the others." Of such checks and balances through the separation of powers be concluded, "To preserve them must be as necessary as to institute them."

"An elective despotism was not the government we fought for; but one in which the powers of government should be so divided and balanced among the several bodies of magistracy as that no one could transcend their legal limits without being effectually checked and restrained by the others." – James Madison, Federalist 84, 1788

"The principle of the Constitution is that of a separation of Legislative, Executive and Judiciary functions, except in cases specified. If this principle be not expressed in direct terms, it is clearly the spirit of the Constitution... "– Thomas Jefferson, letter to James Madison, 1797

James Madison on the need for the "separation of powers" because "men are not angels," Federalist 51 (1788)

We must never forget that the founders understood they had to create a government but also understood the danger of government. "Government, even in its best state, is but a necessary evil; in its worst state, an intolerable one." Thomas Paine

Thomas Jefferson compared government to a fire. He said, "if small contained, and well-tended, it was most useful and beneficial; large, expansive, and neglected, it was most destructive."

The founders understood that this government they must create was also the single biggest threat to that freedom they had just won. In order to preserve that freedom for themselves and for future Americans, the founders chose to diffuse power rather than concentrate power in the hands of one or a few.

When we look for the definition of separation of powers we find a common definition such as an act of vesting the legislative, executive, and judicial powers of government in separate bodies. This is an accurate definition so far as the powers that we the people granted to the federal government are concerned. The framers intended an even greater and more meaningful separation of powers than that just between the federal branches. The founders determined that power should also be separated between the federal government and the state governments, thus diffusing power even more.

In the 10th Amendment it was made clear that the federal government was only to have the powers specifically granted by "we the people" to the federal government in the Constitution; those 26 powers. The 10th Amendment states, "The powers not delegated to the United States by the Constitution, nor prohibited by it to the States, are reserved to the States respectively, or to the people."

The founding fathers had good reason to include the 10th Amendment in the Bill of Rights. The issue of power – and especially the great potential for a power struggle between the federal and the state governments – was extremely important to the founding fathers. They deeply distrusted government power, and their goal was to prevent the growth of the type of government that the British had exercised over the colonies.

We must remember that adoption of the Constitution of 1787 was opposed by many well-known patriots including Patrick Henry, Samuel Adams, Thomas Jefferson, and others. They passionately and prophetically argued that the Constitution would eventually lead to a strong, centralized state power which would destroy the individual liberty of the people. Many of this persuasion were labeled "Anti-Federalists."

The 10th Amendment was added to the Constitution largely because of the intellectual influence and personal persistence of the Anti-Federalists and their allies. It's quite clear that the 10th Amendment was written to emphasize the limited nature of the powers delegated to the federal government. In delegating just specific powers to the federal government, the states and the people, with some small exceptions, were free to continue exercising their sovereign powers.

When states and local communities take the lead on policy, the people are that much closer to the policymakers, and policymakers are that much more accountable to the people. Few Americans have spoken with their president; many have spoken with their mayor. Adherence to the 10th Amendment is the first step towards ensuring liberty in the United States; liberty through decentralization.

The separation of powers between the federal and the state government is the greatest safeguard to maintain individualism because the diffusion of power is greatest.

Madison continued in Federalist Paper No. 45:

"The powers reserved to the several States will extend to all the objects which, in the ordinary course of affairs, concern the lives, liberties, and properties of the people, and the internal order, improvement, and prosperity of the State."

The Founders believed very strongly in states' rights because they understood that the surest way to maintain individual liberty was to instill safeguards against centralized power. Not only would establishing several smaller governments (the states) afford people the ability to move elsewhere, but they would also have more of a say in the public affairs of their surroundings. More simply, citizens would be closer to the people who were making decisions on their behalf.

The second way in which the founders intended to diffuse power and maintain freedom and liberty was to create three branches of federal government with specific duties, functions, and authority. The three branches were independent branches but were within the same government and must function together. The founders, in order to maintain as much independence as possible, incorporated a system of checks and balances between the three branches.

It was to these three powers that Jefferson was referring when he said the powers must maintain their mutual independence, so the government will last long. It is interesting that Jefferson, an Anti-Federalist, did not include in this statement anything about the maintenance of rightful powers given to the federal government and state governments; federal government was given 26 enumerated powers and state governments all other.

Article 1, Section 1., of the United States Constitution states "All legislative Powers herein granted shall be vested in a Congress of the United States, which shall consist of a Senate and House of Representatives."

This means that congress is the only part of the government that can make new laws, change existing laws or abolish existing laws. If the Judiciary, through rulings or otherwise, were to make law, change existing law, or abolish existing law, the Judiciary would be infringing on the power of the legislative branch of government. As Jefferson said the Judiciary would then not be maintaining its mutual independence and the longevity of our nation would be threatened.

If the Executive branch through regulation or executive order were to make law, change existing law, or abolish existing law, the Executive branch would be infringing on the power of the legislative branch of government. As Jefferson said the Executive branch would then not be maintaining its mutual independence and the longevity of our nation would be threatened.

Article 2, Section 1., of the United States Constitution states, "The executive Power shall be vested in a President of the United States of America. He shall hold his Office during the Term of four Years, and, together with the Vice President."

To have executive power would give you the power of enforcement and administering the law as called for by the law itself. The executive branch has the requirement to enforce all laws and each law, in its entirety. The executive was not granted the freedom to pick and choose which laws they would or would not enforce or which part of a law they would or would not enforce. If the executive were to choose not to enforce certain laws, or choose to enforce portions of a law and not the whole of the law, that executive would be assuming the legislative role by effectively nullifying a law duly passed by the legitimate law-making branch.

In addition, the executive branch is not given the power to change law or to nullify law through regulation or through executive order. This is also assuming the power of the legislative branch and assuming legislative power.

If the Legislative branch, through any action other than that of legislating, were to administer the laws it had passed, it would be assuming the power of the executive branch and infringing on the power of another branch.

If the Judiciary branch were to require the Executive branch, through any ruling, to administer a law not in accordance with the written law, or to perform a function outside of its explicit constitutional duties, the Judiciary branch would be usurping the power of the executive branch.

Article 3. Section 1. of the United States Constitution states, "The judicial Power of the United States, shall be vested in one supreme Court, and in such inferior Courts as the Congress may from time to time ordain and establish."

Alexander Hamilton wrote in Federalist 78 that the Judiciary branch would be the least dangerous branch to the Constitutional rights. This is because the Judiciary has no influence over either the sword or the purse. It even depends on the aid of the executive for the efficacy of its judgements. Liberty has nothing to fear from the judiciary alone, but everything to fear from it union with either of the other branches.

Very early in our existence as a free and independent people, based on the principles of individuality, our founding fathers prophetically wrote about the collectivist encroachment on those liberties through the very branch of government that was supposed to be the least dangerous of all; the Judiciary branch.

"At the establishment of our constitutions, the judiciary bodies were supposed to be the most helpless and harmless members of the government. Experience, however, soon showed in what way they were to become the most dangerous; that the insufficiency of the means provided for their removal gave them a freehold and irresponsibility in office; that their decisions, seeming to concern individual suitors only, pass silent and unheeded by the public at large; that these decisions, nevertheless, become law by precedent, sapping, by little and little, the foundations of the constitution, and working its change by construction, before any one has perceived that the invisible and helpless worm has been busily employed in consuming its substance. In truth, man is not made to be trusted for life, if secured against all inability to account." Thomas Jefferson- Letter to Monsieur A. Coray, October 31, 1823

"The Constitution . . . meant that its coordinate branches should be checks on each other. But the opinion which gives to the judges the right to decide what laws are constitutional and what not, not only for themselves in their own sphere of action but for the Legislature and Executive also in their spheres, would make the Judiciary a despotic branch." John Adams in a letter to Abigail Adams (1804)

The idea of having power diffused between the federal government and the state governments, and then to have the federal power diffused between three branches of government with checks and balances one against the other, was because the founders understood the evil of government. Men are not angels. Many men lust after power. Government is comprised of those who lust after power. Government, by its very nature seeks more and more power.

Consequently, the founders did everything they could to prevent the concentration of power. We know this based on what the founders told us.

"It is the duty of the patriot to protect its country from its government."—Thomas Paine

"Government is not reason, it is not eloquence, it is force; like fire, a troublesome servant and a fearful master. Never for a moment should it be left to irresponsible action."—George Washington

"Experience hath shewn, that even under the best forms of government those entrusted with power have, in time, and by slow operations, perverted it into tyranny."—Thomas Jefferson

Separation of Power, was one of the defenses the founders used to protect us from that biggest threat to our freedom that was necessary for them to create; government. The founders set up the safeguards so that freedom, liberty, and individualism, could be maintained and prevent the encroachment of collectivism or tyranny.

The structure of our government is very complex. Power was designed to reside primarily in the people, then the states, and lastly the federal government. Within the federal government we were given three branches of government and within the legislative branch we were given two independent houses that operate under their own rules. The founders did not intend for it to be easy to "get things done in Washington." The founders clearly understood that every time a law was passed, a regulation or executive order was written, or a ruling was given by the courts, we the people lost a little bit of our freedom.

It was the intent of the founders that any form of infringement on our freedom, a law, a regulation, an executive order, or a ruling, received a close review and that infringement had received a full course of due diligence. It was also the intent of the founders that when a law was passed in congress, the law was established by the actions of congress and not left to be determined through regulation by the executive branch. The founders certainly had complete faith that those passing laws to infringe upon the freedoms of the people would take the time to read and understand the bill and not "pass it so they find out what was in the bill away from the fog of the controversy." This, the founders would have considered a severe dereliction of duty, a violation of the oath of office, and an action paving the road for oppressive government or tyranny.

The founders clearly intended that all law must be passed by congress even if they did not act in a time frame prescribed by the executive or for that matter act at all. If the executive determined it was the responsibility of the executive branch to enact law because congress did not, that executive would be usurping the power of the legislative branch and acting outside the purview of the United States Constitution. That executive would be violating the constitution and paving the road to oppressive government or tyranny.

The founders clearly intended that all law must be passed by congress. The founders did not give the Judiciary branch of government the power to enact a law based on some perceived implied freedom within the United States Constitution. The founders did understand that times would change and that changes might have to be made to the constitution which would change the law. The founders provided a means to amend the constitution. It was their intent that these changes in the constitution or the law be made by those means and not by the ruling of some unsubscribed number of supreme court justices. If the justices determined it was in their purview to change the essence of the constitution based on their own judgements, they would be violating the constitution and paving the road to oppressive government or tyranny.

Separation of government or the different power centers of government is essential to maintaining the special gift of freedom and liberty won by our founders and bequeathed to future generations of Americans. The founders paid the price to be free. They understood that if freedom was to be maintained, future generations would have to have that same burning desire to be free that they had. That burning desire exemplified by, "give me liberty or give me death."

Today we have less freedom than we had yesterday, and we certainly have less freedom than we had in 1789. That freedom has been squandered and a major reason for this squandering is that we the people have allowed the federal government to violate the 10th Amendment time after time. In addition, we have allowed the legislative branch to abdicate its power of being the sole legislative body and consequently the most powerful branch of government, by allowing both the executive branch and the judiciary branch to become the originator of law.

Congress has for years passed laws that were at best outlines of their intent. They would place all the detail of the law in the hands of the executive by stating within the law that the specific details would be outlined in regulations written by the different departments and agencies of the executive branch. To legislate does not mean to pass ideas or headlines. A law depends on the details. Laws are passed, and the public does not have any idea what the impact of the law is for several years; the pubic must wait for the regulations to be written.

In today's America, it is common to hear the public declare that the executive should change this, or they should change that. The American public, along with the executive have declared, that if congress will not act then the executive has the duty and the responsibility to act. This is in direct violation of the United States Constitution.

In today's America, it is commonly heard that the Supreme Court has issued a ruling and therefore their position is the law of the land. This is also in direct violation of the United States Constitution. The Judiciary has no power to legislate. The rulings of the court are to be considered only that, rulings and not law. Court cases are initiated for the sole purpose of eventually having the Supreme Court rule on a case and in effect have the Supreme Court rewrite a law that was duly passed and signed into the law per the details of the United States Constitution.

Our road is being paved to oppression and tyranny due to the powers not maintaining their mutual independence. The Federal government has discarded the 10th Amendment. The Federal government has assumed powers far and beyond the 26 powers granted to it by we the people. Many within the government and many citizens of the United States believe the power of the Federal government has no limitations. This is the definition of oppression and tyranny.

The executive branch has assumed the power granted to the legislative branch. Many within the executive branch of government and many citizens of the United States believe that the executive branch has all power through the power of the "phone and pen." The executive branch has even determined it is within their power to perform a very specific power given to the legislative branch, and that is to declare war. Such concentration of power is paving the road to oppression and tyranny.

It was the Judiciary branch that was thought to be the least significant branch of the three branches of government. Their specific duties were outlined in Article 3, Section 3, of the United States Constitution:

The judicial Power shall extend to all Cases, in Law and Equity, arising under this Constitution, the Laws of the United States, and Treaties made, or which shall be made, under their Authority;-to all Cases affecting Ambassadors, other public ministers and Consuls;-to all Cases of admiralty and maritime Jurisdiction;-to Controversies to which the United States shall be a Party;-to Controversies between two or more States;-between a State and Citizens of another State;-between Citizens of different States;-between Citizens of the same State claiming Lands under Grants of different States, and between a State, or the Citizens thereof, and foreign States, Citizens or Subjects.

In all Cases affecting Ambassadors, other public Ministers and Consuls, and those in which a State shall be Party, the supreme Court shall have original Jurisdiction. In all the other Cases before mentioned, the supreme Court shall have appellate Jurisdiction, both as to Law and Fact, with such Exceptions, and under such Regulations as the Congress shall make.

The Trial of all Crimes, except in Cases of Impeachment, shall be by Jury; and such Trial shall be held in the State where the said Crimes shall have been committed; but when not committed within any State, the Trial shall be at such Place or Places as the Congress may by Law have directed.

These limited powers that were extended to the Judiciary have now extended to the Judiciary becoming the most powerful, most political, and least accountable branch of our government. Rulings are declared to be law. The courts have not only assumed all power over both the legislative branch and executive branch, but have also now assumed the role of the Creator. Courts have assumed they understood better what the intent of a law was despite what the written words stated. Courts have assumed they know the intent of written documents because they understand the motives of the writer despite the actual written words. The courts have assumed they are not just Courts of Law, but they have divine powers. This is paramount to despots who declared their word was law because they were as one with divinity.

A free and independent nation based on the principles of individualism require power to be defused and not concentrated. A collectivist nation (Marxist, Communist,

Socialist, Progressive, Liberal) requires concentrated power because a collectivist nation demands total conformity. The more and more concentrated power in the United States has become, the less and less free the people have become. The government is more and controlling the "lives and thoughts" of the people. The road to oppression and tyranny is being paved by accumulating power in the hands of fewer and fewer.

Chapter 8. RULE BY THE PEOPLE

In September of 1620, 102 passengers boarded a ship known as the Mayflower bound for the new world. The ship was blown off course and the Mayflower landed five hundred miles north of its intended location. Arriving in the wrong place, these people remained aboard the Mayflower while they evaluated their situation. Before they went ashore, the people adopted the Mayflower Compact which provided their laws and how their new colony would be administered. The Mayflower Compact emphasized the concept that government came from the governed, with rights from the Creator, and that the law treated all equally.

As early as 1620, Americans declared that the people were the sovereign and government was the servant. When the Americans declared their independence from Great Britain, 156 years later, they wrote in the Declaration of Independence, "We hold these truths to be self-evident, that all men are created equal, that they are endowed by their Creator with certain unalienable Rights, that among these are Life, Liberty and the pursuit of Happiness. — That to secure these rights, Governments are instituted among Men, deriving their just powers from the consent of the governed." Once again Americans said our rights come from our Creator and not from man, and the government receives its power from the people; the people are the sovereign and the government is the servant.

Eleven years later, these same Americans drafted the United States Constitution that would be the governing document for these now free and independent Americans. These free and independent people began that document with the words, "We the people, in order to form a more perfect union." The Constitution did not begin with We the Government, We the Oligarchs, We the King, We the Emperor, or We the Czar. The first words in the Constitution, We the people, means that it is the people who are sovereign, and the government is the servant.

Two years later the states were given the first amendments to their new constitution. The people began the process of ratifying these amendments to become a part of the Constitution. These ten amendments became known as the Bill of Rights. The colonists said, it is these rights outlined in these ten amendments that are never to be taken from the people. The 9th amendment was as important as any of the others. The 9th amendment reads, "The enumeration in the Constitution, of certain rights, shall not be construed to deny or disparage others retained by the people."

The 9th Amendment's purpose is very clear. The Bill of Rights mentions certain rights that are to be protected from government interference; these rights include freedom of speech, freedom of religion, freedom of the press, freedom of assembly, and the right to keep and bear arms, among others. Just because a right is not mentioned in the Bill of Rights, that does not mean that the government automatically has the right to interfere with it. Instead, the 9th Amendment says that any right not enumerated, or listed in the Constitution, is still retained by the people. It means that there are other rights that people have that are not listed in the Constitution. The Founding Fathers realized that they could not possibly list every natural right of human beings that needed protection. Instead, they delegated certain powers to the government that were specifically spelled out in the Constitution, and said everything else is left up to individuals and to their state governments. The people are in all cases to be the sovereign, and the government is in all cases to be the servant.

What does it mean to be sovereign? Sovereignty is defined as 1. the quality or state of being sovereign, or of having supreme power or authority. 2. the status, dominion, power, or authority of a sovereign; royal rank or position; royalty. 3. supreme and independent power or authority in government as possessed or claimed by a state or community. (1)

It was commonly thought that to be a sovereign you must be a monarch; a king, queen, or other supreme ruler, or a group or body of persons or a state having sovereign authority such as an oligarchy. This was the common order prior to the American colonies; that is that an individual or small group was held to be sovereign and the people were the servants or subjects of such sovereign. In all of these collectivist situations, the rights of the individual were always subordinated to whatever the sovereign determined was for the good of the collective. Individuals who did not conform to these demands were considered to be a rebel and were punished severely, up to and including death.

The idea of popular sovereignty, or the sovereignty of the people's rule, is the principle that the authority of a state and its government is created and sustained by the consent of its people, through their elected representatives, but the people remain as the source of all political power. This is what the Mayflower Compact introduced to the American colonies.

The founders, in the Declaration of Independence, The United States Constitution, and the Bill of Rights declared that the United States of America would be a nation with the people as the sovereign and those in government would be the servant. This was the opposite of what the world knew at that time. People were to be servants to the King, Emperor, or Czar. Our founders told the whole world that the idea of sovereignty in the hands of one or a few was not the way the United States would operate. They said the people will be sovereign and it would be governments purpose to serve the people. Truly, the principle of individualism, at its very core, was introduced to the world.

Thomas Jefferson explained why this was so important to protecting freedom when he said, "When governments fear the people, there is liberty. When the people fear the government, there is tyranny. The strongest reason for the people to retain the right to keep and bear arms is, as a last resort, to protect themselves against tyranny in government."

Popular sovereignty expresses a concept, individualism, and does not reflect or describe collectivism. Under the individualist concept, people have the final say in government decisions. Benjamin Franklin expressed the concept when he wrote, "In free governments, the rulers are the servants and the people their superiors and sovereigns"

The United State of America was founded as an individualist nation where individual rights are paramount, property is that of the individual and not the state, and everyone has the right to pursue their own happiness, strive to reach their full potential, achieve their dreams, be self-reliant, and live as a free and independent individual. The individual would not have to, nor would they be expected to limit their dreams and desires, even if the collective or the sovereign would disagree with those dreams or desires of the individual and those dreams or desires were deemed by the collective or the sovereign not to be in the best interest of the collective. The individual's achievements or desire to achieve would also not have to be limited, even though they were deemed to be detrimental to the ego or self-image of others.

When the sovereigns of Europe and elsewhere in the world heard that the upstarts in the American colonies believed people could and would rule themselves, these sovereigns scoffed at the naïve upstarts. The sovereigns disdainfully looked at the colonies and stated that the idea of popular sovereignty was only a dream and would fail. The sovereigns explained, because they knew, that a successful sovereign must be very involved in and interested in the functioning of their kingdom. If, and when, a sovereign was no longer actively involved or no longer interested in the functioning of their kingdom, another aspiring sovereign would take advantage of that non-involvement and disinterest and would suddenly, through revolution, or gradually, through fundamental transformation, become the sovereign and the former sovereign would become the servant.

Today, in America, in many areas of our lives, we the people are no longer the sovereign. In an individualist nation, where the people are the sovereign, the individuals own the property. This is opposed to a collectivists nation where it is considered that all is owned by the sovereign and/or the collective, be it productive property or otherwise. It was determined in Jamestown, that in America it would be the individuals who would be in ownership of both productive property and other property to be disposed as the owner saw necessary.

It was Karl Marx, in the mid 1800's, that told the collectivist that all property, productive or otherwise, was the property of the state. Anything the individual claimed to own was only theirs on loan and must eventually be returned to its rightful owner, which is the state or collective. Marx said this should be done by implementing a steeply progressive income tax and a 100% death tax. The state or collective would then determine how these confiscated assets should be redistributed to the others in the collective. Marx stated all redistribution should be based on need and that need would be defined as what was in the best interest of the collective.

The United States adopted an income tax in 1913. At the time it was adopted the top rate was 7%. The collectivists, to have the income tax amendment ratified, promised that the predominant 1% rate, and the top rate of 7%, would be the rates for years, yes even decades to come. The Income Tax Amendment, or Government Confiscation of Private Assets Amendment was ratified in 1913. Before the end of Woodrow Wilson's first term in 1917, the top rate had been raised by almost 10 X's to 67%. The governments sovereignty over the private assets of the citizens had begun. Today it is common to hear collectivists refer to taxes on a basis of how much people should be allowed to keep and not how much people should be forced to pay. The implication is that all income is the government's and they will determine what the individual can keep for their needs.

Today the government imposes an Estate Tax or a Death Tax on what an individual has accumulated up to the time of their death, just as dictated by Karl Marx. However, the rate paid by those the deceased has named in their will is not 100%. The rate has fluctuated over the years and has been in the high 70% range for much of its time in existence. The collectivist believes that an Estate Tax or Death Tax is very fair because it is simply a return of assets that the individual has unjustly accumulated anyway, to the rightful owner of everything, the state or government. The collectivist believes that the rightful owner, the state or collective, can then redistribute these assets as they determine is in the best interest of the collective. When we the people accept that the government is the rightful owner of our property, we have abdicated our role as sovereign and accepted a role of servant. We have abdicated our right to individualism and accepted that our individual rights should be subjugated to the good of the collective.

A sovereign controls the servant while the servant is reliant on the sovereign for their wellbeing. A kind and considerate sovereign is a benevolent sovereign while a harsh and demanding sovereign is often referred to as a tyrant. Whether benevolent or a tyrant, they are still sovereign, and the people would still be servants. Our founders understood that if the United States was to remain a free and independent nation, the sovereign people would have to be self-reliant as opposed to government reliant, the people would have to be responsible for their actions, and the people would have to understand that it is their actions and decisions that are the cause of the outcome, good or bad. The people would have to not only assume the title of sovereign, they would also have to accept the responsibility.

The collectivist or socialist method of some working and others receiving based on need, or as Karl Marx stated, 'From each according to his ability, to each according to his need" does not work. The Americans learned this as early as 1608 in Jamestown. Perhaps, Captain John Smith was the first American anti-collectivist when he told the other early Americans, "He who will not work, will not eat." I would imagine the rest of Captain Smith's talk probably went like this, "If we are going to survive and then prosper, all will have to be self-reliant, all will have to be responsible, and all will have to be productive. All will have to be responsible individualists for the collectivist method we tried has failed and we will all perish unless we change now. From now on each individual will be the beneficiary, good or bad, of their own effort, their own ingenuity, and their own imagination. Reward will not be determined by the collective based on need, but your reward will be on your shoulders. We are no longer a collectivist group, but we are individuals working to better our own lot, which history will show will better the lot of all."

Thomas Jefferson is credited with saying, "The democracy will cease to exist when you take away from those who are willing to work and give to those who would not."

While living in Europe in the 1760s, Benjamin Franklin observed: "in different countries ... the more public provisions were made for the poor, the less they provided for themselves, and of course became poorer. And, on the contrary, the less was done for them, the more they did for themselves, and became richer."

"The government of the United States is a definite government, confined to specified objects. It is not like state governments; whose powers are more general. Charity is no part of the legislative duty of the government." -James Madison, Jan. 10, 1794 (speech before the House of Representatives)

Here is some of what James Madison, the author of the United States Constitution, said about the General Welfare Clause of the Constitution; the clause loved by the collectivist.

“With respect to the two words ‘general welfare’ I have always regarded them as qualified by the detail of powers connected with them. To take them in a literal and unlimited sense would be a metamorphosis of the Constitution into a character which there is a host of proofs was not contemplated by its creators. If the words obtained so readily a place in the Articles of Confederation and received so little notice in their admission into the present Constitution, and retained for so long a time a silent place in both, the fairest explanation is, that the words, in the alternative of meaning nothing or meaning everything, had the former taken for granted.”

What Madison said is that if the federal government has not been given the power to do something by the Constitution, they cannot use the “general welfare” clause as a justification for doing it. In other words, you cannot use the General Welfare Clause to exceed the enumerated powers of the Constitution. Madison also said that if one were to choose between the General Welfare Clause meaning everything or meaning nothing, it means nothing.

The founders understood the necessity for the sovereign of this country, the people, to be productive and self-reliant sovereigns. Alexander Hamilton famously said, "When the people find that they can vote themselves money, that will herald the end."

Never did the founders intend that our nation would become a collectivist nation where the government would assume authority over all assets and then determine to redistribute those assets through a welfare state and/or safety net system. We were specifically told not to do this because it would be the end of freedom and liberty. The founders understood that if the government were to assume control over all property and assets, they, the government, would have assumed the role of sovereign and the people would have been relegated to the role of servant. The people of the United States would no longer be a free and independent people, they would be slaves to the state, no longer self-reliant but government reliant. When we the people choose to receive a dole from government, we are assuming the role of servant and accepting the government as sovereign. We are choosing collectivism over individualism.

We the people, or we the sovereign did give the federal government limited power over commerce. The Commerce Clause describes an enumerated power listed in the United States Constitution (Article I, Section 8, Clause 3). The clause states that the United States Congress shall have power "To regulate Commerce with foreign Nations, and among the several States, and with the Indian Tribes."

The Commerce Clause has been used by the collectivist through the federal government to control individual businesses that the federal government has come to deem would have an effect on interstate commerce. Madison intended that the Commerce Clause would have a much more limited role than the collectivist has assumed. Madison said:

“For a like reason, I made no reference to the power to regulate commerce among the several states. I always foresaw that difficulties might be started in relation to that power which could not be fully explained without recurring to views of it, which, however just, might give birth to specious though unsound objections. Being in the same terms with the power over foreign commerce, the same extent, if taken literally, would belong to it. Yet it is very certain that it grew out of the abuse of power by the importing states in taxing the non-importing, and was intended as a negative and preventative provision against injustice among the states themselves, rather than as a power to be used for the positive purposes of the General Government, in which alone, however, the remedial power could be lodged.”

Madison said that the Commerce Clause was inserted in the Constitution not to allow the federal government to control interstate commerce, but to allow the federal government to control the states should the states interfere in interstate commerce – big difference.

Although the term capitalism was hardly used at the time we became a free and independent state, the founders supported the principle of economic liberty underlying it along with individualism. The founders understood that property rights and free markets were the basic elements of what it means to be free. They therefore believed that government has a responsibility to protect the rights of all to participate in the economy by upholding contracts, lifting artificial trade barriers, and protecting the right to acquire, possess, and freely use property.

The founders did not, however, advocate a completely "laissez-faire" economic policy, since they understood that the government had a role to play—a limited role—in regulating the economy. For example, at the time of the founding, the government inspected goods that were imported into the United States. They created licensing systems for certain professions. Mostly they understood it was the role of government to provide a free-market economy by expanding the opportunity for all to participate in the market; the Declaration of Independence did state that all have the right to pursue happiness, even if the happiness pursued was in commerce.

In a collectivist society, the economy is centrally planned by the government. The government controls and regulates every aspect of commerce. The United States today, at best would be classified as a mixed economy. The government

(Federal, State and Local) controls or partially controls goods or services, such as education, courts, roads, hospital care, and postal delivery. The federal government provides subsidies to agricultural producers, oil companies, financial companies, companies in the energy industry, and utility firms. Private individuals cannot legally provide or purchase certain types of goods without governmental permission.

In the U.S., private businesses need to register with government agencies, and many types of professionals can only operate with government-approved licenses, including funeral attendants, auctioneers, private investigators, makeup artists, hair stylists, real estate agents, and financial advisers.

Every type of business and every form of economic exchange is affected by government policy. The Food and Drug Administration (FDA) must approve consumable foods and medicines before they can be sold and requires producers to provide very specific disclaimers. Businesses can only advertise their goods and services if they comply with the Federal Trade Commission (FTC). The hiring, compensation, and firing of employees must comply with the Fair Labor Standards Act (FLSA), the Employee Retirement Income Security Act (ERISA) and many other regulations from agencies such as the Department of Labor (DOL).

Even Saturday afternoon street corner stands operated by children, who might be selling lemonade, homemade cookies, or pretty rocks, are subject to regulations and are closed and in some cases fined because they did not comply with government regulations. The government has become sovereign over the economy and is today telling individual owners how they must operate their businesses. The more power the government assumes over commerce, the more the United States becomes a collectivist nation and the closer we become to a fully centralized and planned economy.

The federal government acts like it stands as sovereign in the American system, probably because it does, even though it was never intended by those who created the government. In fact, the federal government was never meant to serve as anything more than an agent, exercising the specific powers delegated by the true sovereign – the people - and enumerated in the Constitution.

I believe it is fair to say that today most Americans believe it was the intent of the founders that the federal government should be at the top of the power pyramid. These Americans would be shocked to learn that what they were taught is wrong; It was the intent of the founders to have the federal government at the bottom of the pyramid. Under the intended constitutional system, "we the people" were to hold the top position of authority, with the states under us, and the federal government would be supreme only within the limited scope of the explicit powers delegated to it.

The very first words of the Constitution made this clear. "We the people," appear in large, ornate letters. This is because, when an 18th century British king issued a grant, his name always appeared at the top in the same fashion. The framers merely replaced the king's name with "We the People," signifying the sovereign authority from which the delegation of power flowed.

So, the ultimate and final authority was to always remain with the people. The states were also supposed to hold an important position, with the federal government being the most limited in power and lowest on the power pyramid. In a collectivist structure, the federal government would be most powerful and at the top of the pyramid, with the state's a distant second, and "we the people" would be the servants at the bottom of the pyramid structure.

The European sovereigns explained, because they knew, that a successful sovereign must be very involved in and interested in the functioning of their kingdom. If, and when, a sovereign was no longer actively involved or no longer interested in the functioning of their kingdom, another aspiring sovereign would take advantage of that non-involvement and disinterest and would suddenly, through revolution, or gradually, through fundamental transformation, become the sovereign and the former sovereign would become the servant. Those European sovereigns were very prophetic. We the people are abdicating our sovereignty due to non-involvement and disinterest.

(1) www.dictionary .com

Chapter 9. MARXIST INFLUENCE

Collectivism is a political theory associated with Marxism, Communism, Socialism, and Progressivism. More broadly, it is the idea that people should prioritize the good of society over the welfare of the individual. Collectivism always puts what is presented as being in the best interest of the collective before what the individual determines what is in the best interest of the individual. Collectivism is the opposite of individualism which favors independent and self-reliant individuals.

Ayn Rand defined collectivism as, "Collectivism means the subjugation of the individual to a group -- whether to a race, class or state does not matter. Collectivism holds that man must be chained to collective action and collective thought for the sake of what is called 'the common good'."

The goal of the collectivist is to have a society where there is equality in all areas of life – economic, social, and political. The collectivist believes there should only be one class in all areas and says if there is only one class, then society is truly a classless society, economically, socially, and politically. Because there is only one class, and the good of the collective is always placed ahead of the individual, all people will conform to the ways of the collective.

To be totally equal economically, the collectivist says that nobody can be rewarded on production. Everybody must be rewarded on need. If producer A produces five times more than producer B, but producer B has himself and four dependents and producer A has only himself as a dependent, producer B will receive five times what producer A would receive. Under the collectivist scenario all would then be economically equal.

To be totally equal socially, there would only be one class and thus there would be a classless society. All productive property would be owned by the state so all of society would be workers. The collectivist also says that most of social stratification comes about because of economic stratification, and because that does not exist, all in society would be equal.

To be totally politically equal, there would be no royalty, no nobles, and no permanent elected or autocratic class. Those performing administrative duties for the collective would be rewarded based on their need. The opportunity to accumulate through graft and corruption would be eliminated. The only purpose to be a part of the administrative class would be to truly serve, so goes the theory.

The collectivist also says that a totally classless society allows each person to pursue their own interests since they would be rewarded based on need regardless of production or contribution. The collectivist believes that because each person is contributing to society based on their passion, they will perform to the best of their ability. The need for what the collectivist calls the greatest divider, competition would be negated. Collectivists have referred to competition as the great contributor to inequality.

In the world of the collectivist, those who are passionate about commerce, will produce to the maximum of their ability because their productive contribution is in the best interest of the collective. If producer A produces to his maximum capacity, he will be greatly rewarded psychologically because he understands it is his financial production that allows the painter to create to their maximum potential, the writer to create to their maximum potential, the poet to create to their maximum potential, or the street performer to entertain to their maximum potential. In this world it is believed, that with no competition for monetary gain or for individual recognition, all will perform to their maximum potential; the collective will operate at its maximum potential because all will strive for the best for the collective and not for the best of the individual.

The collectivist understands that to reach this sought after classless society, actions will have to be taken. In general, the activist has stated a revolution will have to occur, or in absence of a revolution a fundamental transformation that gradually changes an individualist society into a collectivist society will have to be forged. It was always understood by the collectivist; the Marxist, the Communist, the Socialist, and the Progressive, that this transformation would be difficult, and it would suffer setbacks along the way. Throughout the years, the collectivist has understood that they would have to employ deceit, cunning, and even use ruthless and tyrannical methods of persuasion. The axiom of the collectivist has always been, "the ends justify the means."

To bring about this classless society that is totally equal and totally conforming, the collectivist knew it would require economic changes as well as societal changes. We have already discussed some of the economic changes the collectivist said had to come about. Two key economic areas are the implementation of a steeply progressive income tax along with a steep, preferably 100%, death tax.

Other economic changes the collectivist knew they had to bring about was a totally government controlled lending system. This would mean that the federal government would not only regulate, but would have a total monopoly on the lending system. The collectivist understands that another very useful way to redistribute wealth is to lend money to those who cannot repay or show no desire to repay and then forgive the loan. The private capitalist had to be banished from lending because the capitalist based their lending decisions on ability to repay, willingness to repay, and true value of collateral held as security for the loan. The collectivist understands that sound lending principles are not conducive to the principle of redistribution.

Full and complete government control over production of all goods and services, or central planning, is also an economic requirement of the collectivist. When business planning is in the control of private ownership, private ownership produces based on the profit principle. Private business will produce based on demand of the public for certain goods and will invest funds in innovation based on perceived desires of the public. The collectivist believes that production for profit is not necessarily in the best interest of the collective nor is innovation based of perceived desires of the public in the best interest of the collective.

The collectivist believes that a group of central planners, who have the perceived needs and not the desires of the public as its gauge for production and innovation, better serves the collective. Therefore, the collectivist believes that all production and innovation should be controlled and dictated by the central planners who are needs oriented, as opposed to profit minded private board rooms. During the transformation period, central planning is enhanced by government regulation and by the government picking winners and losers through loans, grants, and tax credits. It is also enhanced by the government assuming control through direct ownership or regulation.

The collectivist has as a primary goal to destroy society, so it can be rebuilt to bring about their classless society that is totally equal and totally conforming. The collectivist understands that to accomplish their goal, more than economic tactics must be used. The collectivist understands that a direct assault on society itself must be launched. This direct assault on society will be accomplished on three primary fronts; one, by tearing down all long-standing principles, morality and religion;

two, by destroying the fundamental unit of a strong individualist society, the family; and three, by transforming the education system into an indoctrination tool.

The destruction of all long-standing principles has been undertaken primarily by belittling and denouncing the two biggest threats to collectivism; the Bible and the United States Constitution. The United States Constitution is the ultimate law in the United States. Despite the collectivist arguments being made today, the United States and its Constitution were founded on Biblical principles. The founders recognized in the Declaration of Independence that the fundamental rights of man in a free society are rights given by the Creator and not by government or man. The collectivist, at their basic core, disagree with this critical principle of the United States foundation. The collectivist believes that man or government is the ultimate grantor of basic rights. The collectivist argues that since government or man grants the rights they have the right to withdraw these basic freedoms.

A free society, or an individualist society depends on and requires diversity of thought. A free society or an independent society requires freedom of political thought and the ability of that thought to be expressed through free speech and free assembly. A free society, or an individualist society requires that both extremes of the political spectrum exist and that both can freely express their ideas. This is in complete contrast to the demands of a collectivist society that requires total conformity in all thought, political, social and economic. The collectivist therefore must destroy or at least minimize the Constitution and the Bible upon which the long-standing principles of the United States and the Constitution are based.

Specifically, the collectivist will discredit the American Constitution by calling it inadequate, old-fashioned, and out of step with modern needs. And they will discredit the American Founding Fathers by presenting them as selfish aristocrats who had no concern for the "common man," and by belittling all forms of American culture and discouraging the teaching of American history on the grounds that it was only a minor part of the "big picture."

The abolition of or neutralizing of morality in a collectivist society goes hand in hand with the outlawing or minimizing of religion in society. In a collectivist society there is no right or wrong, there is no black or white, there is no good or bad. All collectivist societies have minimized or outlawed the Bible. The Bible teaches that sin or wrong doing is not relative to what others are doing or what feels good for a person. All collectivist societies become either atheist or secularist.

Today, anybody who professes the teachings of the Bible is ridiculed, discriminated against, and limited as to where and how they can practice their faith. Two practices of the collectivist have come to dominate not only American society, but all Western society and those practices would be moral relativism, and political correctness. Both practices are strongly advocated by atheism and secularism; if it feels good than do it.

Moral relativism is often described as the position that moral or ethical propositions do not reflect objective and/or universal moral truths, but instead make claims relative to social, cultural, historical or personal circumstances. Moral relativism is simply the view that moral judgments are true or false only relative to some standpoint and that no standpoint is uniquely privileged over all others.

This is in direct contrast to the teachings of the Bible. Not only does the Bible teach that there is right or wrong, good or bad, and there are absolutes, but it teaches that consequences exist for the decisions and choices that are made. The Ten Commandments were given as a critical guide for society to understand what right or wrong, or good or bad is. Many nations, including the United States have based their criminal and moral codes based on the Ten Commandments. The collectivist, being threatened by right or wrong, good or bad, is striving to eliminate the Ten Commandments in any and every form from our society.

The definition of politically correct would be conforming to a belief that language and practices which could offend political sensibilities should be eliminated. This conforms to moral relativism in that we avoid terms that would define right or wrong, good or bad, by substituting some other term considered to be non-judgmental such as undocumented for illegal.

Here are some additional examples of political correctness in the United States today:

All U.S. government agencies are now banned from producing any training materials that link Islam with terrorism. In fact, the FBI has gone back and purged references to Islam and terrorism from hundreds of old documents.

Authorities are cracking down on public expressions of the Christian faith all over the nation, and yet atheists in New York City can put up an extremely offensive billboard in Time Square during the holiday season that shows a picture of Jesus on the cross underneath a picture of Santa with the following tagline: "Keep the Merry! Dump the Myth!"

More than 75 percent of the babies born in Detroit are born to unmarried women, yet it is "politically incorrect" to suggest that there is anything wrong with that.

The number of gay characters on television is at an all-time record high. Meanwhile, there are barely any strong Christian characters to be found anywhere on television or in the movies, and if they do happen to show up they are almost always portrayed in a very negative light.

Specifically, the collectivist was directed to abolish morality and religion by eliminating all laws governing obscenity by calling them "censorship" and a violation of free speech and free press; by breaking down cultural standards of morality by promoting pornography and obscenity in books, magazines, motion pictures, radio, and TV; by presenting homosexuality, degeneracy, and promiscuity as "normal, natural, healthy;" by infiltrating the churches and replacing revealed religion with "social" religion, by discrediting the Bible and emphasize the need for intellectual maturity, which does not need a "religious crutch;" and by eliminating prayer or any phase of religious expression in the schools on the ground that it violates the principle of "separation of church and state."

The core unit which determines the strength of any society is the family. A society with strong family units has historically benefited economically and morally. Studies have shown that the proportion of married parents in a state is a top indicator for economic outcomes. The share of married parents is generally a stronger predictor of economic mobility, child poverty, and median family income. Also, crime is far lower in states with a greater share of married-parent families.

The traditional family unit provides many other economic benefits, including accumulating more wealth than those in other household types, having more assets and enjoying higher levels of income, and are thus less likely to be poor. Children from married-parent households are more likely to receive human capital to help them thrive in the world. They have access to greater levels of income and parental attention and are less likely to be abused or neglected. Strong families reduce the likelihood that youth will participate in delinquent behavior, thus contributing to a lower crime rate and a higher academic performance as well as a higher rate of participation in extra-curricular school activities.

Perhaps more important to freedom and liberty, families are a source of emotional support, love, security, and protection. Healthy family relationships result in happy and secure children who are willing to explore different thoughts and ideas. These children will generally be secure enough to question, but not disrespect, authoritarian figures such as teachers and police.

The love and support of family members motivates children to continually strive to achieve and to be better citizens. The development of strong moral character in a child is perhaps the most important benefit of a healthy family to a free and independent society. It is the family that provides guidance to children regarding values, discipline, and the internal code of conduct that motivates human behavior. A similar belief system can also encourage each family member to pursue his own interests while adhering to a strong set of personal beliefs and expectations. Children that have been raised in strong traditional family units are more likely to be independent and self-sufficient.

Independent and self-reliant citizens, that question authoritarian figures and have learned to do independent research and thinking, are essential for a free and independent society or a society built on individualism, but they are problem citizens for a collectivist society that requires citizens willing and eager to conform to a single avenue of thought. In any society that is becoming or has become a collectivist society, the achievers and the independent thinkers are always eliminated. Those who would question and think for themselves are quickly labeled as undesirables and trouble makers.

Collectivists have openly called for the abolition of the family. Not only did Marx and Engels call for the abolition of the family, but many of the nineteenth century socialists such as Charles Fourier and Robert Owen also promoted the abolition of the family unit. The abolition of the family unit by the collectivist takeovers in the twentieth century would decrease the influence of the family unit. The idea of it taking a village or a state to raise a child was widely promoted. In the collectivist state, the child is considered property of the state, as opposed to a member of a family, and the education or indoctrination of the child is deemed to be solely that of the state.

The collectivist state, by diminishing the role of the family in the raising of the child, not only is able to indoctrinate the child with the collectivist idea of total conformity, but the child is also raised to believe that it is the state to whom total allegiance is given. Children are taught it is their duty to spy on any and all family members and report any disloyalty, perceived or real, to the authorities. The indoctrination of the child includes the belief that the greatest achievement for which they should strive, is to be loyal members of the state, subjugating any individual desires or goals to what the state tells them is in the best interest of the collective.

Specifically, the collectivist was instructed to discredit the family as an institution, encourage promiscuity and easy divorce, emphasize the need to raise children away from the negative influence of parents, and attribute prejudices, mental blocks, and retarding of children to the suppressive influence of parents.

The collectivist has believed that public education is a critical element in transforming society. We saw this as one of the critical elements Karl Marx and Friedrich Engels said was essential to transform a free and independent society to a totally equal and conforming classless society. Many in education in the Untied States agree with Marx and Engels and support using the collectivist ideology of Marx and Engels in the education, or indoctrination process.

Sarah Knopp is co-editor of "Education and Capitalism: Struggles for Learning and Liberation" (Haymarket Books, 2012) and also teaches government and economics and is an activist in United Teachers Los Angeles. She has said that Marxism must be used to craft a plan of action and an alternative vision of education. She went on to say that social justice educators must be "transformative intellectuals" who wield a working-class liberatory pedagogy. The conclusion at which she arrived was that schools will not be able to satisfy expectations without a revolutionary transformation of the economic and social system in which they operate.

And all along we thought the purpose of education was to teach reading, writing, arithmetic, accurate history, civics, and thinking.

Education should be defined as a means of developing knowledgeable, well-rounded individuals who can think critically, process information, make good decisions, and support themselves. To educate means to challenge a student by defining a problem and then requiring that the student research the problem and arrive at a solution. Indoctrination is defining the solution and then requiring the student to support the already defined solution. Education does not impose restrictions on research with a predetermined ideology while indoctrination is the imposition of an ideology as the solution in all circumstances.

"Crimes of the Educators" by international journalist and educator Alex Newman, reveals how the architects of America's public-school disaster implemented a plan to socialize the United States by knowingly and willingly dumbing down the population:

"We need to draw a clear, defining line between education, which enables people to know how to think, versus what the government is doing today, which is indoctrination, training people what to think rather than how to think and how to process information and how to have critical thinking ability," Newman explained.

The public education system is too far gone to be saved, Newman argues, largely because progressive educators such as John Dewey designed it specifically to dumb down and indoctrinate children. Therefore, he says modern education reformers need to start over if they wish to save the system.

"If we're going to have government-provided education, we really need to start from the very beginning, from the very foundation and build on a new foundation that's based on proper reading, proper writing, and real knowledge – not indoctrination," Newman said. "And for that to happen, we've got to start from scratch and we've got to build from there, because the system, I think, is too far gone, it's too corrupt to be salvaged."

It's possible for publicly educated children and adults to overcome the indoctrination, Newman asserted, but it's very difficult.

"If you subject yourself to a government school or you subject your children to a government school, you're automatically starting with a huge handicap because a government school is scientifically designed to dumb you down," he said. "And it is possible to bypass that, but it takes very, very hard work."

Those wishing to overcome the dumbing-down process need someone who can teach them to read properly, according to Newman. Once they can read well, they can acquire knowledge and truth independently and receive a real education.

"You're not going to get the truth out of the government schools any more than you're going to get the truth from the far-left media," Newman warned.

He offered further advice for adults wishing to educate themselves: Read books.

"They hide all the secrets in the books," he quipped. "Get books. Make sure you have a big library stocked with information on everything you need to know: history, economics, politics, culture, science – we all need to be well-rounded people, and if we're going to educate others, we need to be educated ourselves.

"So, there's a lot of great sources out there, but I really recommend people just need to expand their libraries, get off Facebook, turn off the TV, and educate yourself with books the old-fashioned way. I think there's really no shortcut."

Specifically, the collectivist was directed to get control of the schools, use them as transmission belts for socialism and current Communist propaganda, soften the curriculum, get control of teachers' associations, and put the collectivist party line in textbooks. In addition, the collectivist was instructed to use student riots to foment public protests against programs or organizations which are not conforming to the collectivist ideology.

Chapter 10. HELP FOR COLLECTIVISTS

Broadly defined, individualism emphasizes personal freedom and achievement. Individualists believe in recognizing and rewarding the individual for personal accomplishments such as important discoveries, innovations, great artistic, athletic, or humanitarian achievements, business achievements, and all actions that make an individual stand out from the group. Collectivism, in contrast emphasizes embeddedness of individuals in a larger group. It demands conformity and punishes individuals from dissenting and being different from the standards of the collective.

The collectivist views the productive individual with suspicion and disdain. The collectivist will shame the achiever and demand that the achiever shares what the collectivist has defined as surplus, with the community. Collective punishments exist to penalize the achiever. These punishments take the form of social ostracism, loss of status, steeply progressive taxation, and even violence.

So successful has the collectivist been in his demonization of the achiever, that many who profess to be individualists, use the same tactics of suspicion and disdain for individuals who have achieved more than they have. Many who profess to be individualists, but support a collectivist agenda, will distinguish themselves from the collectivist by not advocating as rapid a transformation to collectivism as does the openly proclaimed collectivist.

The collectivist has been so successful advancing their belief that achievement is harmful to the collective, that those who believe in and advocate for individual achievement are deemed to be extremists by much of society. An extremist is somebody who is labeled as having fanatical political and social views. Collectivists will commonly refer to anybody who disagrees with them, especially an individualist, as a Nazi, an extremist, a racist, a sexist, Islamophobic, and xenophobic. When a person, because of a constant barrage by the collectivist press, becomes thought of as being one of these politically incorrect terms, they can be and often are harmed politically, socially, and economically. Many staunch individualists, and virtually all partial individualists will do anything to avoid these false and misleading labels.

It is common political practice, and has been for many decades, perhaps even as much as the last century, to have politicians who claim to be individualists, promote and vote for collectivist programs and ideals. It is very uncommon on the other hand, to find collectivists promoting or voting with individualist programs and ideals. The collectivist press is very unforgiving. The collectivist programs and ideals have been sanctioned by the collectivist press as being politically correct. It has only been in the last ten years or so that an individualist press with any voice or impact has been in existence.

It is for these reasons we have witnessed the growth of spurious individualists as well as weak or easily persuaded individualists. Consequently, some individualists have in many situations become an ally to the collectivist in the collectivists quest to transform the United States from a nation based on the individualist belief to a nation based on the collectivist doctrine. The collectivist has a long-term goal. Typically, the collectivist will start the negotiations from an extreme position. The collectivist will then moderate his position while at the same time beginning his onslaught of name calling and demonizing the individualist for not being willing to compromise. The collectivist knows their position will be advanced with any compromise by the individualist because his fundamental transformation of the United States has been advanced, and the individualist has been demonized and his belief system minimized.

The collectivist has been told that an important aspect of the fundamental transformation to a totally conforming and equal society is that all borders should be obliterated and there should be free and unencumbered movement by all. This is critical to the transformation because it will lessen the allegiance of the people to a particular national state and bring about a globalist oriented world. The collectivist has been told that his allegiance should be to the collectivist doctrine and not to a specific nation. The more open the borders become, the less nationalistic the people will be.

Open borders are also critical in the quest of the collectivist to redistribute wealth from the more advanced and wealthier nations (often referred to as imperialist nations by the collectivists) to the less developed nations. This redistribution of wealth between nations is as critical to the collectivist as is the redistribution of wealth between what he terms the top 1% and the rest.

Borders, and the protection of those borders against invaders, have traditionally protected the safety of the people within a nation as well as protecting the culture of the people within the nation. Nations have passed laws to protect themselves and their culture. The concept of "rule of law" would dictate that the immigration laws of a specific nation be upheld and enforced. The collectivist is unable to advance their agenda if "rule of law" is upheld and enforced and open borders become closed borders.

To the collectivist, the concept of "rule of law" impedes their march to their fair and just classless society that is totally conforming and totally equal in all areas. The collectivist has come to completely ignore the laws that require immigrants to enter a country legally by refusing to protect boarders, by refusing to require that people in their country illegally be removed, and by openly encouraging illegal immigration and aiding and protecting the illegal immigrant.

The spurious individualist has aided the collectivist in their desire to open all borders. The spurious individualist has publicly stated that they support enforcement of all immigration laws, including closing borders, but they refuse to vote for funding to close borders, they refuse to enforce deportation claiming it is cruel and inhumane, and they advocate for legalizing illegal immigrants because it is the easiest course of action even though it violates the laws of the land. The spurious individualist refuses to adhere to "rule of law" and joins the collectivist in supporting "arbitrary law" in their quest to aid the collectivist and be politically correct.

The weak individualist also aids the collectivist in encouraging illegal immigration and ignoring "rule of law." The weak individualist will take a stand advocating following the law by enforcing border security and deporting illegal immigrants under certain circumstances such as the illegal has committed a violent illegal act within the nations borders. What the weak individualist refuses to acknowledge is that the illegal immigrant was a criminal within the borders even before they committed any illegal violent act. The illegal immigrant is a criminal because they violated the nation's immigration laws.

Because of the constant barrage of the collectivist demanding that political correctness be employed, the weak individualist has already publicly proclaimed that the illegal immigrant is not really a criminal, but they are simply undocumented. The weak individualist is more concerned that they be deemed to be politically correct, so they are not demonized and labeled as racist, as full of hate, and as being completely void of having any compassion for the poor, for women, and for children. The weak individualist takes the stance that the right to adhere to “arbitrary law” and void “rule of law” this time is okay because all people must show compassion. The weak individualist then demands that in the future they will insist on adhering to “rule of law” because it is essential if we are to remain a free and independent nation.

In both situations, the collectivist, with the aid of those who claim to be individualists, has moved forward their long-term goal of destroying the concept of “rule of law,” a concept that truly is essential for a free and independent society to exist, thrive, and grow. In both situations the collectivist, with the aid of those who claim to be individualists, has advanced the requirement of open borders to fundamentally transform a free and independent nation to a collectivist society that is a classless society, totally conforming and totally equal.

Benjamin Franklin stated, "When people find that they can vote themselves money, that will herald the end of the republic." The people did find that they could vote themselves money by electing people to positions of power who advocated the collectivist concept of sharing the wealth, and it has heralded the end of a free and independent nation. This redistribution comes under the pretense of being a safety net as a part of the welfare state. The safety net is comprised of a collection of services provided by the state including welfare, unemployment benefits, universal healthcare, homeless shelters, subsidized services such as public transport, and other means of wealth redistribution. The safety net concept brings about a welfare state which is a system based on the assumption by a political state that their primary responsibility is to provide for the individual needs and social welfare of its citizens.

The collectivist concept embraces the safety net and welfare state completely. An ideal collectivist society would receive all the Gross National Product of a society and then redistribute that Gross National Product based on what it determines to be in the best interest of the collective and on what the state defines would be the needs of the individual. The individualist believes the safety net system and the welfare state are detrimental to promoting self-reliance, they destroy ingenuity and innovation, they are a breeding ground for poverty, crime, and corruption, and they always herald the end of a society based on freedom and independence.

The individualist embraces the concept of self-reliance, not only of the individual but also of society. The individualist believes that self-reliant individuals are more prone to be law-abiding citizens, more concerned about maintaining themselves, their property, and public property, and more concerned about and thus more involved with their children, their children's education, and their children's morals and behavior. The individualist understands that a society comprised of self-reliant individuals will be a society concerned with helping a neighbor or a friend that has come upon difficult times, with maintaining a law-abiding society that adheres to "rule of law," and with providing quality education for children that focuses on teaching children how to think and act independently and understanding what it means to be a good citizen because they have been taught by example.

The individualist embraces a charitable safety net system. A charitable safety-net system is critical to maintaining a free and independent society. A charitable safety net system gives aid and assistance through the good will and charity of individuals and not through the confiscation of private assets by the government and then redistributed as the government deems appropriate. A charitable safety net system encourages the individual who has fallen on hard times to become self-reliant because they understand they cannot rely on the charity forever. The person who has fallen on hard times must take positive action to improve his position, so they can become self-sustaining and not a burden to society or a slave to the state. The person who has been helped than assumes their responsibility to help others when they fall on hard times.

The collectivist does not want the person who has fallen on hard times to become self-reliant. The collectivist wants that person to become a ward of the state and a slave to the collectivist. The more wards of the state the collectivist creates, the greater is the need for a state run safety net system and a large welfare state. This insures power, both financial and political, to the collectivist politician and heralds the end of a free and independent society by transforming society to a classless society that is totally conforming and totally equal.

Both the spurious individualist and the weak individualist have been complicit in assisting the collectivist in this endeavor. The collectivist has employed their typical tactics of demeaning and demonizing those who oppose their ideals by their typical name calling and political correctness ploy. The collectivist has been so successful in their implementation of the safety net system and welfare state mentality that it is commonly believed that the United States has a constitutional duty to provide these state benefits through their redistribution system. The weak and the spurious individualist no longer debates if these benefits are constitutional or not, but what they debate is what is the best way to administer these collectivist programs.

When a spurious individualist unveiled his long-awaited anti-poverty agenda as part of his "Better Way" initiative, he expressed what were, to true individualists, familiar misgivings about the welfare state. It was expensive. It was bureaucratically complex. It had failed to conquer poverty. Yet the report of this spurious individualist also took as a given that "repairing the nation's safety net" in order to "cure poverty and prevent it" was the responsibility of the federal government.

In a significant sense, one could say the collectivist had won: Even those who referred to themselves as individualists were arguing about the best way to fulfill the national government's responsibility for the material well-being of the populace, but not about whether it bore that responsibility or constitutional authority. Yet, at least theoretically, many individualists would revolt at hearing the idea so starkly expressed. That tension between theoretical concerns about the welfare state and, in practice, an acceptance — even embrace -- of one of the collectivists primary requirements, by a self-proclaimed individualist, to fundamentally transform a free and independent nation to a classless society that is totally conforming and totally equal using the safety net system or welfare state. The collectivist movement was advanced far beyond what any collectivist could have done.

The collectivist wants all to believe that it is the responsibility and duty of the federal government to repair the nation's safety net in order to "cure poverty and prevent it." The federal government was not given the power by "we the people" to do either. Our founders clearly understood the threat to the freedom they had just won and understood that freedom would cease to exist if the government determined it was their duty and responsibility to "cure poverty and prevent it". It was Jefferson who told us that freedom and independence would cease to exist if the government would take from those who would work and give to those who would not. A government safety net requires that the government redistribute wealth. The redistribution of wealth is the reason freedom and independence will cease to exist. Any educated person, not an indoctrinated person, understands that poverty cannot be cured, and it cannot be prevented except under the ideal collectivist scenario. History has shown that under the ideal collectivist scenario, all become poor. 'Poverty stricken' is a relative term. Under the collectivist scenario, the living standard for all, except the new government class, declines below what was considered "poverty stricken" prior to when the collectivist scenario existed. Crime, corruption, famine, and sickness all increase. History has shown this to be true in every transformation, whether through revolution or transformation.

The collectivist has been told that to advance the fundamental transformation to their desired fair and just classless society that is totally conforming and totally equal, government must be expanded. The citizens must learn to depend on the state and look to it for all their needs. Only a big government, the collectivist states, is capable of benefiting the collective as a whole and minimizing the negative affect the nonconforming or achieving individual will have on total conformity and total equality.

The individualist believes, along with the founding fathers, that government is the single biggest threat to freedom and independence and therefor must be limited to performing only the powers given to it in the United States Constitution. Alexander Hamilton said, "It's not tyranny we desire, it's a just, limited, federal government."

And Thomas Jefferson explained why limited government was critical to preserving freedom and independence when he said, "Experience hath shown, that even under the best forms of government those entrusted with power, have, and in time, and by slow operations, perverted it into tyranny." The collectivist understands that to bring about his tyrannical fair and just classless society will take time and it will be done gradually. The collectivist was even told that they will be assisted in this transformation by "useful idiots" who are in fact spurious individualists and weak individualists. The collectivist has as a goal to grow the federal government in numbers of bureaucrats as well as dollars confiscated from citizens and spent by government in comparison to the Gross Domestic Product.

Here is a history of Federal Spending since our Founding:

Federal spending in the first half of the 19th century stayed typically below 2 percent of GDP except in wartime. In the Civil War, federal spending exploded to 13 percent of GDP. After the Civil War spending gradually declined. It dropped below 4 percent of GDP in 1872 and below 3 percent of GDP in 1880. Thereafter, federal spending hovered between 2.5 percent and 3 percent of GDP until World War I. Federal spending peaked at 24 percent of GDP and declined below 4 percent in the 1920s. Federal spending reached 10 percent of GDP in the 1930s before rocketing to 48 percent of GDP at the end of World War II. From the end of World War II to the mid-1980s federal spending gradually increased from 15 percent to 22 percent and then declined to below 20 percent of GDP by 2000. Since 2000 federal spending has slowly increased as a percent of GDP, with a blip to 24 percent GDP in the aftermath of the Crash of 2008. (1)

With the increase in government spending, government has become more intrusive in the lives of Americans. Our government is truly out of control. The Administrative Conference of the United States lists 115 agencies in the appendix of its "Sourcebook of United States Executive Agencies," but notes: There is no authoritative list of government agencies. For example, FOIA.gov [maintained by the Department of Justice] lists 78 independent executive agencies and 174 components of the executive departments as units that comply with the Freedom of Information Act requirements imposed on every federal agency. This appears to be on the conservative end of the range of possible agency definitions. The United States Government Manual lists 96 independent executive units and 220 components of the executive departments. An even more inclusive listing comes from USA.gov, which lists 137 independent executive agencies and 268 units in the Cabinet. In truth, nobody knows the actual number.

Consequently, the Federal Government has truly come to control the lives and interests of "we the people." This is in direct contrast to the specific intent that the United States Constitution was intended to accomplish. The original intent by the founders was that "we the people" would be protected by the Constitution. Patrick Henry stated, "The

Constitution is not an instrument for the government to restrain the people, it is an instrument for the people to restrain the government - lest it (the government) come to dominate our lives and interests."

The collectivist has been helped by the "useful idiots" (spurious individualist and weak individualist) in this expansion of government. Under our current federal budget law, the amount of money a federal agency will automatically get for the next year is based on the current year's amount, plus inflation, which is the "baseline" for the next budget year. No agency head is required to justify their need for the increase. When a proposal is made to give the agency less than the projected increase, the collectivist screams that necessary government spending is being cut, when in fact, the proposal still increases the actual dollar amount to the specific agency. The spurious individualist and weak individualist, after being demonized by the collectivist, has consistently acquiesced to the demands of the collectivist.

The United States Constitution Article 1 Section 7 of the United States Constitution states: "All bills for raising Revenue shall originate in the House of Representatives; but the Senate may propose or concur with Amendments as on other Bills." This is straight forward. Bills dealing with raising money must originate in the House, but the Senate does have input. It is fair to say that since raising revenue is all part of the budget process, bills proposing a budget should start in the House.

The same article and section goes on to state: "Every Bill which shall have passed the House of Representatives and the Senate, shall, before it become a Law, be presented to the President of the United States; If he approves, he shall sign it, but if not, he shall return it, with his Objections to that House in which it shall have originated, who shall enter the Objections at large on their Journal, and proceed to reconsider it." Hence the president is involved in passing the budget as well, since his signature is required for it to become law along with the approval of both the House and Senate.

The final paragraph of the section goes on to say: "Every Order, Resolution, or Vote to which the Concurrence of the Senate and House of Representatives may be necessary (except on a question of Adjournment) shall be presented to the President of the United States; and before the Same shall take Effect, shall be approved by him, or being disapproved by him, shall be repassed by two thirds of the Senate and House of Representatives, according to the Rules and Limitations prescribed in the Case of a Bill." It is clear both houses of the Congress and the president must be and are involved in passing a budget.

For the past several years, the Constitution was ignored by Congress and the President. Between fiscal year 1977 and fiscal year 2015, Congress only passed all twelve regular appropriations bills on time in four years - fiscal years 1977, 1989, 1995, and 1997. During the last several years, at least the last six, no budget was passed. Congress and the

President ignored their constitutional duties and passed and signed massive continuing resolutions. The spurious individualists and weak individualists agreed to these violations of the Constitution and law, which always led to increased spending and more government.

Under the leadership of a spurious individualist, recently a budget was finally passed. This budget was passed by a group of collectivists, spurious individualists, and weak individualists with no support from true individualists because the budget completely met all the demands of the collectivists. In typical fashion, the head of the spurious individualists explained that it was in the nation's best interest to cave to the collectivists, but that they had set the stage to bring about true individualist policies in the future. Once again, the spurious individualists and weak individualists promoted the collectivists agenda of fundamentally transforming the United States from a free and independent nation to a fair and just classless society that is totally conforming and totally equal by making our massive government even more massive.

Time after time, we have witnessed the spurious individualist and the weak individualist assist the collectivist in destroying the freedom and independence our founders entrusted with us to keep. The fair and just classless society, the one that has failed every time it has been tried, is consistently advanced as much by the spurious individualist and the weak individualist as it is by the collectivist. Consequently, the principles of rule of law, limited government, divided government, and rule by the people are constantly and consistently minimized. Our founders knew these principles are essential to a free and independent people. Collectivists understand these principles are in direct contrast to bringing about their ideal fair and just classless society that is totally conforming and totally equal. The collectivist has understood these principles must be destroyed. The collectivist understood the destruction of these principles would take time, and that they would receive some assistance from "useful idiots." The collectivist did not understand, however, just how much assistance they would receive and how simple it would be to coerce that assistance. The collectivist understands he owes these spurious individualists and weak individualist a great deal of gratitude for their overwhelming and sometimes enthusiastic support in bringing about the fair and just classless society that is totally conforming and totally equal.

(1)https://www.usgovernmentspending.com/federal_spending_chart

Chapter 11. THE CHOICE

The fundamental transformation of the United States, as promised, is taking place and has made substantial progress over the last century or so. Remember that fundamental transformation means to transform the United States from a nation founded on the individualist principle, championing rule of law, limited government, divided government, and rule by the people; to a collectivist nation that has as its goal a fair and just classless society that is totally conforming and totally equal. Many individualists, along with many collectivists, believe the transformation has already occurred and there is no turning back. If this is true, then taking the time to write this was a total waste. You, taking the time to read this, will be a total waste. People involved in campaigns of any kind, if they are individualists would be wasting their time. Individualists gathering together to learn and to plan would be wasting their time.

But, an individualist understands that they cannot give up because they can never live a totally conforming and totally equal life. An individualist understands that it is there basic nature to put forth the best effort they can, that they will strive to be the best they can be, that they will never be able to take from others who have worked hard to achieve, and that they must always innovate and achieve. An individualist is driven to do everything they can to leave a free and independent nation to future Americans. Our founders believed in the values of individualism. They were individualists. And we individualist today have that same overwhelming desire to be free and independent and live in a nation based on rule of law, with limited government, with divided government, and where the people are the sovereign and those in government are the servants.

We can participate in rallies, we can share conservative slogans on social media, we can wave the flag, and we can honor our brave soldiers, but that will not slow down the transformation much less stop it. People ask me every time during the question and answer segment of speaking engagements, what we individualists can do to regain and then preserve freedom and independence for those future Americans. Invariably they will have begun their question with a phrase something like, "we do not have a chance, and I fear we are now a minority."

We must remember that the road to gaining and then retaining freedom and independence is difficult because it is a steep and rocky road. The road to tyranny is simple because it is a flat and paved road. All the people must do to enable the establishment of a tyranny is to step aside, let the crowd pass, and then follow. We learned in the American Revolution that attitude and desire were the precepts to gaining freedom and independence. It was the attitude of the Revolutionary leaders that led to the birth of the United States of America.

"They tell us, sir, that we are weak; unable to cope with so formidable an adversary. But when shall we be stronger? Will it be the next week, or the next year? Will it be when we are totally disarmed, and when a British guard shall be stationed in every house? Shall we gather strength by irresolution and inaction? Shall we acquire the means of effectual resistance by lying supinely on our backs and hugging the delusive phantom of hope, until our enemies shall have bound us hand and foot? Sir, we are not weak if we make a proper use of those means which the God of nature hath placed in our power." Patrick Henry

"Our cruel and unrelenting Enemy leaves us no choice but a brave resistance, or the most abject submission; this is all we can expect - We have therefore to resolve to conquer or die: Our own Country's Honor, all call upon us for a vigorous and manly exertion, and if we now shamefully fail, we shall become infamous to the whole world. Let us therefore rely upon the goodness of the Cause, and the aid of the supreme Being, in whose hands Victory is, to animate and encourage us to great and noble Actions - The Eyes of all our Countrymen are now upon us, and we shall have their blessings, and praises, if happily we are the instruments of saving them from the Tyranny meditated against them. Let us therefore animate and encourage each other, and shew the whole world, that a Freeman contending for Liberty on his own ground is superior to any slavish mercenary on earth." George Washington

"Liberty must at all hazards be supported. We have a right to it, derived from our Maker. But if we had not, our fathers have earned and bought it for us, at the expense of their ease, their estates, their pleasure, and their blood." John Adams

The founders clearly understood that appeasement was not an answer. They understood that compromise at that stage would only slow the inevitable; that they would be slaves to a tyrannical government. They stated, as you can see above, that was not an option. The only option they had was to act and declare that they would accept nothing less than freedom and independence and refuse the chains of government and tyranny. The Declaration of Independence was signed and, war was declared on Great Britain.

At that time, it is now estimated that 20% of the population was loyal to Britain, fewer than 20% were Revolutionists, and the rest were fence sitters, not interested, or totally oblivious. (1) As was stated before, we know the odds were greatly against the individualists or Revolutionists. The enemy had a powerful Army, the most powerful Navy in the world, and the financial resources to support them. The Revolutionists had a rag tag Army at best, no Navy, and virtually no financial resources to support the rag tag Army much less to build a Navy. The only thing the Revolutionists had favoring them was their attitude and their desire to be free from the chains of government.

The Revolutionists were told they did not have a chance to defeat those who would keep them from being free and independent. The Revolutionists were told they were a minority. There reply was simply, "but we will be free." That is the resolve we individualists who say, we want to be free, must have. It was that resolve and desire that won freedom and independence and it will be resolve and desire that retains it. Just like the Revolutionists had to act and do certain things to get to the day the United States Constitution was officially ratified, there are actions and certain things we individualist must do to restore those great principles of that Constitution; rule of law, limited government, divided government, and rule by the people.

It was Sun Tzu in the "Art of War" that said "If you know the enemy and know yourself, you need not fear the result of a hundred battles. If you know yourself but not the enemy, for every victory gained you will also suffer a defeat. If you know neither the enemy nor yourself, you will succumb in every battle."

We must understand who we are, and we must understand who the collectivists are. Throughout these pages the contrast between what an individualist believes and what a collectivist believes has been drawn. There is no way that the complete differences could be explained in these few pages, just like there is no way a few slogans, sound bites, or talking points can explain the differences. The differences are great. The basic philosophies are diametrically opposed. The beliefs as to how society is to function is diametrically opposed. Individualists believe in freedom, independence, and encourages self-reliance, while the collectivist believes in government control, dependence, and government reliance. The capabilities and resourcefulness of humans is encouraged and adhered to by individualist while the collectivist discourages these attributes and punishes those who would employ them. The collectivist has learned that in order to advance their cause they must be deceitful, manipulative, and lie, while the basic nature of the individualist insists they be truthful and forthright. These differences, and so many more, must be understood by individualist warriors, just like the Revolutionists understood why they were willing to die for freedom and why they were not willing to have Britain keep them enslaved.

The only way to gain this knowledge is by reading and studying not only the individualist philosophy, but also the collectivist philosophy. It is important to read about the individualist philosophy by those who profess it and by those who oppose it. It is important to read about the collectivist philosophy by those who profess it and by those who oppose it. It is important to read history, but while reading history, it is critical to read authors with different philosophies. By studying in this way, a person learns why they believe what they do and why they do not support the other viewpoint. It is only when a person truly understands the viewpoint of both sides that they can learn to plant seeds when necessary, water and cultivate when necessary, and when the opportunity to harvest presents itself, then harvest.

The person who engages in this type of study and research also learns the end result of each philosophy. The collectivist society is a totally conforming and totally equal society. It is described as a society that has only one class and therefore it is a classless society. Because it is totally conforming, thoughts and actions that are different from what the collective dictates, are not tolerated. Those who would challenge the dictates of the collective are warned that what they are doing is detrimental to the good of all and must be stopped. Those who would continue to challenge, history shows us, are berated, expelled, and finally eliminated.

The classless society is also a society that is totally equal socially, politically, and economically. History has shown that this total equality in reality does not exist even in an aspiring classless society. The social, political, and economical strata are adjusted with the ruling class becoming the top class in all three categories and everybody else falls into the lower class. History also shows us that the lower class becomes a very poor class as economic activity slows, necessary essentials become scarce, crime increases, and dissatisfaction with the government increases. As dissatisfaction increases, the government becomes more tyrannical and despotic.

History also shows us that these collectivist societies become closed societies. News and contact from the outside is curtailed and in many cases completely closed. Immigration and emigration are curtailed and closely controlled. Purges and arrests of those deemed to be enemies of the state become common. History is rewritten, the press becomes controlled, speech is limited, censorship is employed, and any worship of God is outlawed. The collectivist society, which is called a classless society that is totally conforming and totally equal becomes a closed society.

The individualist society can only exist if the society is completely open. Freedom of religion, freedom of speech, freedom of thought, freedom of assembly, and freedom to petition the government must exist. If any of these freedoms are curtailed, then the individualist society begins a transformation to a collectivist society which inevitably becomes a closed society.

An individualist society must protect the speech and thought of all. It is critical to an individualist society that the political fringes exist. This is critical because it requires the society to constantly evaluate itself concerning the principles necessary to a free and independent society; rule of law, limited government, divided government, and rule by the people. Without the fringes challenging society, society will become complacent and the principles essential for freedom will began to be transformed.

History has shown that an individualist society is a society that enables and encourages social, political, and economic mobility. People are not relegated to a position in life determined by birth, by society, or by government, but only by their own decisions and choices. Competition is encouraged and championed. Accomplishment is recognized and appreciated. Individualist societies are societies where economic classes do exist. But history has proven that with the rich getting richer because of effort, innovation, and accomplishment, all of society is benefited and the standard of living for all increases. History has also shown that economic mobility is a reality, with rags to riches stories abundant.

History has shown that inventions and discoveries are greatly enhanced as people are encouraged to learn, to think outside the box, to experiment, and to not quit in their quests because of setbacks. Crime is reduced, poverty is reduced, curiosity is enhanced, and the society becomes an open society, communicating freely and openly with other societies and nations. History has shown that the end result of an individualist society is the opposite of the end result of a collectivist society.

The United States began as an individualist nation. The foundation for us becoming an individualist nation was laid in the first permanent English colony in America at Jamestown, and then at Plymouth. The principles of individualism and the principles of freedom and independence were solidified and codified with the adoptions of the Declaration of Independence, The United States Constitution, and the Bill of Rights. Attacks against individualism and freedom and independence began soon thereafter but were greatly enhanced at the beginning of the twentieth century.

It is critical that Americans understand our founding principles. It is critical that Americans understand the transformation currently taking place and what the outcome will be if that transformation continues. Only if Americans understand this, can they decide and determine if they wish to continue with the transformation to collectivism or if they want to return to an individualist nation.

Americans must also understand that the simple and easy road to take would be to continue the road to collectivism. No changes would have to be made. There will be little or no controversy. On the other hand, the road to reverse the current trend and start to restore individualism and the principles of freedom and independence will be difficult. There will be a great deal controversy. Those who are on the side of individualism, freedom, and independence will be facing great odds. They will be demonized, ostracized, expelled, and yes even eliminated for their beliefs and for their efforts.

After sacrificing much and putting forth a great deal of effort, success is not guaranteed. Our founders faced exactly the same situation. So much did they desire to be free and independent, they chose to move forward, despite the odds and the cost. We must determine if we are willing to proceed despite the odds against success. We must determine if we are willing to proceed despite the cost. We must determine if we desire and love freedom and independence as much as our founders did.

If our nation is to once again become the free and independent nation our founders began and set the foundation for that freedom and independence to be available for all future Americans, we must stop the collectivist movement and began the return to establishing individualism, rule of law, limited government, divided government and rule by the people. In order to stop and then reverse the destructive and enslaving movement of collectivism we have to go to the core of the American people.

This effort must begin today, and it must be done by us. We must begin by planting seeds in the minds of those around us. Discussions must be initiated by us around the kitchen table with our family members, in the coffee shops with our friends and acquaintances, and in other group settings. It is critical as to how we approach these discussions. If these discussions become arguments, we have lost that battle. If these discussions become dialogues by us, we have lost that battle. If these discussions end with us "telling those collectivists just how things are," we have lost that battle.

We individualists must understand that primarily, in these settings, we are simply planting seeds of freedom and independence in the hearts of Americans. History proves that our position is right (correct). Even though we are right (correct) does not mean the collectivist will accept it because we said it, even if we prove the rightness (correctness) of our position.

The only way we win the war is when the collectivist concludes on his own, with our assistance, that history proves his collectivist philosophy destroys people, enslaves people, and destroys entire societies. In our discussions around the kitchen table, in the coffee shops, and in other group settings, we plant the seed, by using revealing examples and asking questions that will entice the collectivist to search on his own. If we have done our jobs properly, the collectivist will seek answers from us or other individualists. We must always remember that some collectivists can be changed, and others cannot. The problem is, we never know which is which. Use great analogies, ask good and leading questions, and allow the seed you have planted to grow. At times you will be the planter, other times you will do the watering and cultivating, and once in awhile you will be the harvester.

It is because of this process that it is so critical that the individualist knows why they believe in the individualist philosophy, how it works, and why it works. It is also because of this process that the individualist must understand the collectivist philosophy, why it fails, and why people still continue to advocate for a failed philosophy. This is why the individualist must study both individualism, and collectivism. This is why the individualist must study history and understand history.

The communications psychologist, John Marshall Roberts said that there are three ways of converting people to a cause: by threat of force, by intellectual argument, and by inspiration. "The most effective of these methods," Roberts said, "is aligning communication about your cause with the most deeply-held values and aspirations of your friends, relatives, neighbors, and fellow citizens. To get people's total, lasting, and unwavering support, in other words, we should try neither to cajole them judgmentally nor convince them forcefully. We should inspire them toward a vision that they—not we—can really care about."

The quest by the collectivists to capture the American education system and convert it to a system of indoctrination has been very successful. Lenin was able to use people like George Counts do begin and further this critical process. It was Lenin who said that if he had a child for four years he would have him for a lifetime. Many leaders of the Teacher Unions like Jeff Bale and Sarah Knopp, openly state that Marxism must be taught in our schools, that teaching social justice and multiculturalism is essential.

Bale and Knopp co-edited a book entitled "Education and Capitalism Struggles and Learning and Liberation." This is a book of different articles written by different people in education. All of them sing the praises of Karl Mark, Friedrich Engels, Lev Vygotsky, and many other self-proclaimed collectivists. Every individualist who is concerned about the direction our education system is taking, should read this book. The why our education system is being transformed into a collectivist indoctrination system is made obvious.

In the forward to this book, Bill Bigelow was asked a question and his answer is very revealing. Bill Bigelow taught high school social studies in Portland, Ore. for almost 30 years. He is the curriculum editor of "Rethinking Schools" and the co-director of the "Zinn Education Project." This project offers free materials to teach a fuller "people's history."

The question was, "That same introduction to 'Rethinking Our Classrooms' also proclaims, 'classrooms can be places of hope, where student and teachers gain glimpses of the kind of society we could live in and where students learn the academic and critical skills needed to make it a reality.' Can you give a few examples from your experience as a teacher of lessons where you have been able to glimpse this more hopeful society?"

Bigelow answered, "I've been in a number of social justice curriculum groups over the years, and this is the key conundrum that we always return to: how can we teach fully and honestly about the enormity of injustice in the world and yet not totally discourage students? I think that 'hope' begins with students' experiences in the classroom. It seems to me that when students feel themselves changing and growing – which is fundamental to believing in the possibility of a different kind of society. One simple example is giving students a chance to write about their lives and share their stories with one another-encouraging them to offer each other positive feedback and to ask big questions about how our personal stories connect to broader social patterns.

We also need to give students the opportunity to feel themselves as 'activists'-broadly understood. So, for example, when we study about global sweatshops and the exploitation of poor countries and communities around the world, we don't just leave our students with the memory of 'people being treated badly.' We highlight the resistance of workers in the Global South, who themselves are fighting for dignity. It's important that our students realize that people are already fighting for better lives, and our role is simply to do our part in the solidarity.

Role plays can reinforce this, too-putting students in the position of organizers: Industrial Workers of the World members during the 1912 Bread and Roses strike in Lawrence, Massachusetts; student activists in apartheid South Africa, confronting what they called their 'gutter education'; student environmental justice activists today working around climate change issues.

As a component of the global sweatshops unit, I assign students 'making a difference' projects to take their learning outside the classroom in order to attempt to make the world a better place. Students have been amazingly creative-they've written children's books that they've read at middle and elementary schools, they've published poetry in community newspapers, they've made raps and videos broadcast on community stations, they've written letters to policy makers, they've organized educational forums for other students. The point is that as teachers we need to pair our teaching of injustice with opportunities to do something about the injustice. Hope comes from being part of the solution, to paraphrase the Black Panther maxim. And hope comes from recognizing that they are not alone;

that there are people around the world combating despair with activism."

There are two overwhelming observations that must be made. The first observation would be that Bigelow is advocating planting into his students minds all that is collectivism. The second observation would be that what Bigelow is advocating is indoctrination and not education. Bigelow is having his students do these activities to prove his collectivist theory. If Bigelow were educating, he would have the students do the activities and research, so they could reach their own conclusion and support that conclusion.

If we as grandparents, parents, and interested citizens are satisfied with our current school system and the results, there is nothing we should do but sit back and allow the school system to continue to indoctrinate. If we are not satisfied with the school system, and see it as not educating but indoctrinating, if we believe to many students are not learning the necessary skills such as reading, writing, arithmetic, history, civics and thinking; and if we believe far too many of our students are being pushed ahead to meet imposed standards while the student is not learning and is being sentenced to a life of failure, then we must take action.

There are several actions that can and must be taken. The first action is to understand the reason for this problem; and that reason is "we the people." To many grandparents and parents have neglected their roles in raising their grandchildren and children. They have neglected their responsibility to be involved in their children's education by not taking an active role of communicating with and supporting their children's teachers and schools. Instead, they have been too busy to be interested in what theirs children were learning, especially if they were doing their homework, if they were progressing, and if they were behaving. We have been far to quick to blame the teachers and the schools for our children's poor academic performance and for their behavioral problems. Parents today make excuses to not be involved in Parent Teacher Associations, to not attend parent teacher conferences, and to not attend school functions.

To many parents today have welcomed the schools taking over what were always intended to be, and should be the responsibilities of the parent, and that is to teach our children proper behavior, morals, values, respect for others, and those matters regarding sex. The collectivist mentality has always been that the child is the property and responsibility of the state and therefore the academic and social development of any child is the responsibility of the state. As the parent abdicated their role and responsibility, the collectivist was only to happy to fill the void.

In a free and independent society, the school system must be a system of education and not a system of indoctrination. We, the individualists must take back our school system. This can only be done by active involvement. Parents must again assume full responsibility for their children. Individualists must become active members and leaders in Parent Teacher Associations. Parent teacher conferences must become a top priority. Individualists must be involved with their children's homework, not just to help the child but to know what the child is being taught. Individualists must sit in on their child's classes. If the child is not performing academically or is not behaving in class, it is the responsibility of the parent, and thus it is the parent who must take responsibly and work closely with the teacher to solve the problem.

Individualists must become involved in the school district by attending school board meetings and becoming familiar with the workings and the problems facing the district. The individualist must become a positive contributor by supporting programs that support individualism and by intelligently opposing collectivist leaning programs that will lead to less education and more indoctrination. The individualist must support individualists who are on the school board or those who wish to be elected to the school board. The individualist must also be willing to run for school board when they realize they would be the candidate with the best chance of being elected. The individualist community must commit to becoming active and involved in all aspects of the education system. A society can only remain free and independent if the children are being educated to learn and think independently as opposed to being indoctrinated to conform to collectivist thought as Bigelow advocated.

OUR CHILDREN MUST BE TAUGHT HOW TO THINK, NOT WHAT TO THINK.

The Orange County Register (California Orange County) recently reported, "The new consensus is being pushed by, among others, hedge-fund-billionaire-turned-green-patriarch Tom Steyer. The financier now insists that, to reverse our worsening inequality, we must double down on environmental and land-use regulation, and make up for it by boosting subsidies for the struggling poor and middle class. This new progressive synthesis promises not upward mobility and independence, but rather the prospect of turning most Californians into either tax slaves or dependent serfs.

California's progressive regime of severe land-use controls has helped to make the state among the most unaffordable in the nation, driving homeownership rates to the lowest levels since the 1940s. It has also spurred a steady hegira of middle-aged, middle-class families — the kind of tax-burdened people Gov. Jerry Brown now denounces as 'freeloaders' — from the state. They may have access to smartphones and virtual reality, but the increasingly property less masses seem destined to live in the kind of cramped conditions that their parents and grandparents had escaped decades earlier."

This is the result of collectivism as history proves. If California continues its present path, it will continue to deteriorate financially and socially with the complete elimination of a middle class. The reason for this situation in California, and many other areas around the United States, is again because of "we the people." Never forget, that when they who are sovereign are no longer interested or involved in their kingdom, the void of sovereignty will be filled, and those who were sovereign will become servants and slaves to the new sovereign. "We the people," who were sovereign, became to busy with other matters, we were no longer interested or involved in our kingdom, and now we are becoming servants and slaves.

If individualists are to become sovereign again they must become interested and involved. City board meetings and county board meetings must be filled with individualists. Individualists must educate themselves on the issues of the day. Individualists must make positive contributions in these meetings and must intelligently oppose all programs that will advance collectivism. Individualists must actively support other individualists who are running for city and county positions. Individualists must be willing to run for city and county positions.

As individualists become educated on what they believe and why they believe it, as well as becoming educated on what collectivists believe and why it always fails, the individualist will be more and more successful in planting seeds. As the individualist becomes more involved in the school system and city and county matters, their positive influence will become a contributing factor to not only slowing the collectivist movement but reversing that damaging and devastating movement.

The slowing and reversal of collectivism must begin in the hearts of individualists, spread to family, friends, and acquittances, become a factor in their children's education and upbringing, become an overwhelming influence in local school boards, and become a part of every city and county government. The slowing and reversal of collectivism will then spread to state government and very quickly to the federal level.

Those who understand the importance of slowing and reversing collectivism must always have as their ultimate goal to restore to our nation the values of individualism, freedom and independence, and a self-reliant citizenry. The principles upon which our founders built this nation, rule of law, limited government, divided government, and rule by the people must be restored so we current Americans can be free and independent and all future Americans, if they are diligent in retaining these principles, will also live as a free and independent people.

This will not be easy. The odds are against us. But, we must have that same love of freedom, the same desire for freedom, and be willing to do whatever is necessary, just as our founders were. This was exemplified by Patrick Henry when he said, "Is life so dear, or peace so sweet, as to be purchased at the price of chains and slavery? Forbid it, Almighty God! I know not what course others may take; but as for me, give me liberty or give me death!"

We also must understand how our founders overcame the great odds they faced. Sam Adams explained what must be done when he said, "It does not take a majority to prevail... but rather an irate, tireless minority, keen on setting brushfires of freedom in the minds of men."

Every individualist must ask, what course they will take. Every individualist must determine if they will be irate and tireless and set brushfires of freedom in the minds of their families, friends, and acquittances. Every individualist must ask if they are willing to be informed and involved and once again assume the role of sovereign. I believe that the DNA of the individualist says they must be free, independent, and self-reliant. Let us say as did John Paul Jones, "I have not yet begun to fight."

(1)http://www.ushistory.org/us/11b.asp

Bibliography

Bale, Jeff and Sarah Knopp Editors, “Education and Capitalism Struggles for Learning and Liberation” Chicago, Illinois, Haymarket Books, 2012

Clizbe, Kent, “Willing Accomplices” Ashburn, Virginia, Andemca Publishing, 2011

Gorgoglione, Robert D., Sr., “Toward Socialist America Collectivism vs. Individualism” United States 2010

Kengor, Paul, Ph. D, “Takedown” Washington D.C., WND Books, 2015

Puls, Mark, “Samuel Adams Father of the American Revolution” New York, New York

Palgrave MacMillan, 2006

Schweikart, Larry, and Michael Allen, “A Patriot’s History of the United States” New York, New York

Penguin Group, 2007

Taylor, Alan, "American Colonies the Settling of North America" New York, New York,

Penguin Group, 2001

Webster, Mary E, "The Federalist Papers Summaries of the 85 Papers" San Bernardino, California, 2008

West, Diana, "American Betrayal the Secret Assault on Our Nation's Character" New York, New York

St. Martins Press, 2013

About the Author

Don Jans has studied history from a very early age. He gravitated toward Russian history and from there found his way to Karl Marx and the study of Marxism. As Don began to understand Marx and what he taught, it became clear to him why the realities of Marxism are not taught in schools. When he began to speak around the country it also became evident to him that Americans did not understand Marxism, including those who would speak in the standard trite clichés.

Don has written two books on the topic of Marxism. He also writes a blog on his website most every week day. You can find those writings, other articles, and links to different radio programs on which he was the guest. The website is www.mygrandchildrensamerica.com. You can also email him with questions or to contact him for speaking engagements at mygrandchildrensamerica@gmail.com

The two other books Don wrote are;

MY GRANDCHILDREN'S AMERICA – WILL IT STILL BE THE LAND OF THE FREE OR THE HOME OF THE BRAVE

GOODBYE CONSTITUTION FREEDOM AMERICA

Don's books are available on his website www.mygrandchildrensamerica.com,

at Amazon, or at Barnes and Nobel